The Collected Poems of Josie Craig Berry

Collected, Edited, and Introduced

by

Jeanetta Calhoun Mish

MONGREL EMPIRE PRESS
NORMAN, OKLAHOMA, UNITED STATES OF AMERICA

2022

REVISED EDITION, 2025
The Collected Poems of Josie Craig Berry
© 2022 by Mongrel Empire Press

ISBN 979-8-9865764-1-1

Author photos courtesy of the Family of Josie Craig Berry.

Book & Cover Design
© 2023 by Mongrel Empire Press

Mongrel Empire Press
Norman, OK
www.mongrelempire.org

This publisher is a proud member of

[clmp]

COUNCIL OF LITERARY MAGAZINES & PRESSES
w w w . c l m p . o r g

Acknowledgements

The Collected Poems of Josie Craig Berry was created in partnership with her descendants; without their help, this book would not exist.

Keely Record spent many hours perusing microfilm issues of *The Black Dispatch*. She also provided moral support, encouragement, and proofreading assistance.

Kylee George and Kristen Grace assisted with research in Oklahoma City and Norman.

Daniel Simon, Editor-in-Chief of *World Literature Today,* greets with enheartening enthusiasm new discoveries from my ongoing Oklahoma Poetry research project.

The Oklahoma History Center's digital and microform issues of *The Black Dispatch* are essential to this project. The Center for Research Libraries Digital Archives provided electronic issues of *The Black Dispatch* that were not otherwise available online.

The Internet Archive and HathiTrust supplied several items that I could neither discover without their database nor access without their digital documents.

The Hampton University Archives sent documents relating to Berry's studies at the University.

Some information was sourced through Ancestry.com and Newspapers.com.

This revised addition includes three poems that were discovered after the first printing. Textual errors and omissions have been corrected.

—Jeanetta Calhoun Mish, Editor

The Collected Poems of Josie Craig Berry

for Josie
1888-1981

and for her grandson
Crawford Henry Lydle III
1944-2020

Introduction to *The Collected Poems of Josie Craig Berry*

Jeanetta Calhoun Mish

The Project

I've been researching early 20th century Oklahoma poetry for fifteen years, but the writings of Josie Craig Berry are, without a doubt, the most significant literary recovery of the project. Eight years ago, an internet search for "Oklahoma poets," turned up a 1937 anthology entitled *Negro Voices*.[1] I purchased the anthology and found not only Josie but also two other Oklahoma Black poets: Nick Aaron Ford, nationally known as the founder of Black Studies who taught at Langston University from 1937-1944; and Myntora J. Roker, who was born in Arkansas. At some point, she joined her minister-husband, Augustus, in the Bahamas, his native country. They immigrated to Oklahoma in 1919; immigration records entered "Bahamas" as the citizenship for both.[2] Both Ford and Roker were strong poets, but Josie's work captured me.[3] As I read more of her writing, I came to admire her mastery of poetics, her wry sense of humor, her Black feminism, and her unwavering and unapologetic insistence on civil rights.

The Life of the Poet

Josie Craig Berry's birth was recorded in St. Louis on November 17, 1888,[4] but her family says she was born on a riverboat between New Orleans and St. Louis. Her father, Wiley Buford Craig, was working as a cotton sampler in Chalmette, Louisiana

---

[1] Murphy, *Negro Voices*. Beatrice Murphy compiled second anthology, *Today's Negro Voices*, in 1970.

[2] Florida, U.S., Arriving and Departing Passenger and Crew Lists, 1898-1963.

[3] Berry, "And Death Went Down (To James Weldon Johnson)," 13.

[4] St. Louis Birth Registers, 1888-1889.

for William W. Bierce, a well-known cotton merchant. Perhaps her mother, (also) Josie, and her father were traveling for his work. The Craig family lived in Louisiana as late as 1896; her brother, John Bierce Craig, was born in Louisiana in 1896. In 1900,[5] the family was living in Clarksdale, Alabama.

Although most Black people in the South were banned from education until after the Civil War, Josie's mother, born in 1863, and her father, born in 1853, according to the 1900 census had at some point received and education. James and Mary Berry, the parents of Josie's husband, Henry Albert (H. A.), both born in 1850, could read by not write according to the 1880 census;[6] their six-year-old daughter was in school. By 1900,[7] the entire family could read and write and two of their daughters are listed as schoolteachers. It's clear that both the Craig and Berry families valued education and encouraged their children to attend college.

In the July 29, 1939[8] edition of Over My Shoulder,[9] Berry's *Black Dispatch*[10] literary column, she announced her graduation from Langston University, Josie lists her "educational path":

> LeMoyne Institute, a New Orleans Convent, public schools in Mississippi, Mary Holmes Seminary at West Point, Miss., Knoxville College, summer session at Harvard University, extension courses taught by O.U. (Oklahoma University) and Oklahoma City U. instructors, and for the time being at Langston.

---

[5] 1900 United States Census, digital image s.v. "Josie Berry."

[6] 1880 United States Census.

[7] 1900 United States Census, digital image s.v. "Henry Berry."

[8] Berry, "Over My Shoulder," 6.

[9] Hereafter, Over My Shoulder is abbreviated OMS.

[10] For more information on *The Black Dispatch* and its editor, Roscoe Dunjee, see Thomson, "Dunjee, Roscoe (1883-1965)."

During the 1905-06 school year, Josie was in her second year at Knoxville College, in the Normal (teaching) department.[11] Her future husband, Henry Albert (H. A.) Berry was a Junior. In both her third[12] and fourth years,[13] she was a student teacher. Josie graduated in 1908, H. A. in 1907. In June 1909, Josie and H. A. married in Oklahoma City and their first child, Henry Albert, Jr., was born in April 1910.[14]

After graduating from Knoxville, Josie and H. A. attended the Harvard Summer School for teachers. Josie enrolled in "College Entrance Requirements in English for Teachers." H. A. enrolled in "Latin for Teachers."[15] In an April 1938 OMS column dedicated to "The Negro in Literature," Berry writes,

> OMS hopes to get permission to use some of (W. S.) Braithwaite's poems this year. It's been twenty-eight years since my husband and I spent part of our honeymoon in the Braithwaite home just outside the Harvard campus. I remember the poet's devotion to Keats and Rossetti and the beautiful lyrics of his *House of Falling Leaves.*[16]

Josie and Henry were at Harvard's summer school for teachers "twenty-eight years" before the date of her column. It's possible that they could not get housing in Cambridge, so were invited to stay with Braithwaite. In 1913, H. A. served as one of three founding officers of the Oklahoma City NAACP; Josie was one of twenty-eight founding members.

---

[11] "Knoxville College Bulletin," June 1906.

[12] "Knoxville College Bulletin," March 1907.

[13] "Knoxville College Bulletin," March 1908.

[14] 1910 United States Census.

[15] "Harvard."

[16] "OMS," April 2, 1938, 6.

By 1920, Josie and H. A. were both teaching at Douglass School; Josie taught science, H. A. taught English and Latin.[17] Josie taught until about 1931; H. A. taught until he retired, probably in the late-1950s.

In October 1939, Josie was named Dean of Women at Langston University, a position she held until the end of the 1941 semester.[18] From circa October 1942,[19] to at least January 1943,[20] Josie was director of the Ogden, Utah Black USO. By March 1943,[21] she was directing the Junction City, Kansas Black USO. Between 1945 and 1949, she took classes toward her graduate degree in Education at the Hampton Institute. She served as Head Resident for the women's dorms and sponsor of the Hampton Women's Caucus. A 1949 recommendation letter to the University of Oklahoma stated she had withdrawn in August 1949 and that she had completed all required classes for the degree.[22] It is unclear whether Josie was accepted to or attended OU's graduate school in 1949 or later. 1949 was the first-year Black students were allowed admittance to the University.

Josie Craig Berry & Women's Clubs

Berry was an active and respected member of the Oklahoma City Black community. That community was Deep Deuce, which many people know of in

---

[17] When one searches the internet for Josie Craig Berry, most of the hits are for biographies of Ralph Ellison which quote a letter Ellison wrote to Josie in 1937. Henry Berry was Ellison's literature teacher; Josie his science teacher and possibly his poetry mentor. She taught at Douglass School from 1921 to 1931, the year Ellison graduated. The letter is archived in the Western History Collection at the University of Oklahoma.

[18] "College Head," 6.

[19] *The Ogden Standard-Examiner,* "Social Worker," 28.

[20] *The Ogden Standard-Examiner*, "Holliday Season," 9.

[21] Berry, "Minutes of the Junction City, KS USO."

[22] "Hampton."

connection with Ralph Ellison, Charlie Christian, and Jimmy Rushing. Zelia Breaux, Ellison's music teacher, and a fine musician in her own right, is sometimes mentioned. Women were at the heart of the Oklahoma City's Black community and their influence was, in part, due to their participation in women's clubs. The clubs benefitted the woman who participated as well as their community as a whole.

It's impossible to overestimate club women's influence in Black communities. Civil rights activist Mary Church Terrell was the first president of the National Association of Colored Women, and the motto of Black women's clubs, "Lifting as We Climb," is from Terrell's 1902 essay on the community role of educated Black women.

> Lifting as we climb, onward and upward we go, struggling and striving and hoping that the buds and blossoms of our desires will burst into glorious fruition ere long . . . Seeking no favors because of our color nor patronage because of our needs, we knock at the bar of justice and ask for an equal chance.[23]

Clubs were often focused on self-improvement in educational pursuits (literary clubs, for instance), becoming a wise and accomplished homemaker (flower clubs and embroidery clubs). They also worked to keep Black youth morally sound and on a trajectory to finishing high school and going to college. Oklahoma City Black women's clubs worked with—and kept a close eye on— the Taft Training School for Girls.[24]

Josie was active in women's clubs for sixty-four years, 70% her life. Berry, her mother, and poets Nicene Wisener and Harriett Jacobson were among the many who sponsored Oklahoma City women's clubs and helped to organize the Oklahoma

---

[23] "Terrell."

[24] For more information on Black women's clubs of the period, see Strong, "The Origin, Development, and Current Status of the Oklahoma Federation of Colored Women's Clubs."

Federation of Black (Negro) Women's Clubs. Berry served as the Federation's official poet and editor—she was responsible for club notes in *The Black Dispatch,* which had been named the "official organ" of the Federation. Berry also served as the statistician for the City Federation of Black Women's Clubs. She served as the president of the Semper Fidelis and Little Playhouse (theater) clubs. In 1919, Berry's poem, "Song of the Negro Club Women" was adopted as the official song of the Oklahoma Federation of Negro Women's Clubs. She was active in at least fifteen clubs, three of them as late as 1962 when she was 74 years old.[25]

Josie Craig Berry's Literary World

Josie Craig Berry lived a literary life. The evidence for her poetry accomplishments are presented in this collection. However, what is not readily apparent is her activity in Oklahoma literary organizations and her warm friendships and literary relationships with both Black and white Oklahoma writers.

Josie's earliest documented literary activities were through her participation in several literary women's clubs, among them, East Side Culture Club, Shakespeare, Little Playhouse, and the Sepia Poetry Club, which her friend, and fellow poet and teacher, Harriet Jacobson, founded. Berry sponsored The Scribblers, which formed through the consolidation of the Poets Group and the Writers' Group. The group sought out and mentored both young writers and practiced poets in the community. In her Over My Shoulder column, Berry featured young writers such as Freddye Harper Williams, Pauline Brown, Billy Taylor, and Carl Thomasson. Williams started her writing career in the Poetry Club and later had a regular column, "Thinkin'

---

[25] Berry belonged to the following clubs: Silver Thimble Embroidery, Renaissance, the Black YWCA, Semper Fi, Look Out, East Side Cultural, Amicus, Sepia Poetry, Fortnightly, Shakespeare, Cosmopolitan, and Little Playhouse. She was active in Entres Nous, Semper Fi, and Golden Glow Flower clubs as late as 1965.

Through," in *The Black Dispatch*. In 1981, Williams was elected to the Oklahoma House of Representatives and served five terms.[26]

Beginning in 1937, Berry served as a bridge between Oklahoma City's Black writing community and the white writing community. Her outreach was met in kind by white authors such as Kenneth C. Kaufman and her close friend, Louis L'Amour. The Writers Club's first speaker was novelist William Cunningham, at the time the Director of the Oklahoma Writers Project. Other speakers included L'Amour and Zoe Tilghman, a well-known (white) Oklahoma writer and poet who was the literary columnist for *Harlow's Weekly*.

Berry was a board member of the Southwest Writers' Congress and, at their first gathering, presented on fair representation of Blacks in fiction—in her presentation, she said that "the only Negro character in (white) fiction who is "a credit to the race, is the Negro doctor in Sinclair Lewis' *It Can't Happen Here*.[27] Among her fellow Congress organizers were Lynn Riggs and B.A. Botkin. Supporters, attendees, and presenters included Witter Bynner, Paul Horgan, Mabel Dodge Luhan, and Oklahomans Kenneth C. Kaufman, Oscar Ameringer, William Cunningham, George Milburn, Louis L'Amour and Jim Thompson, later known as the author of highly regarded crime fiction. In short, Berry was holding her own among famous literati.

On December 27, 1938, she took young poet Troy Jeter to the Oklahoma Writers Congress in Tulsa. In a story on the 1938 Congress published in *The Black Dispatch* (1938-01-01), the reporter notes that "William Cunningham, Federal Writers' Project head, introduced Mrs. Berry to the principal speaker, Mr. Ralph Bates, as being sponsor of the best organized group of writers in Oklahoma City." She also served on the staff of the *Langston Review*, which released its first issue in 1938.

---

[26] "OK Legislature," 48.

[27] *The Black Dispatch*, "Writers Congress in Session at YWCA," 5.

By May of 1938, Berry was listed as a member of the previously all-white Poetry Society of Oklahoma. During the 1938 Poetry Week (May 22 to 28), Berry, The Scribblers, and the Sepia Poetry Club collaborated with the Oklahoma Poetry Society to host James Weldon Johnson who was in town to give the Douglass High School graduation address. Berry and the Sepia Poetry Club prepared a series of radio programs on KOCY. The radio programs included a "brief sketch" of the Sepia Poetry Club and The Scribblers, a history of Black poetry, readings by local Black writers, and a presentation of Johnson's work read by local Black writers. He also attended a Sepia Poetry Club meeting.[28] On May 28, Johnson presented his own work on WKY radio, Oklahoma's largest broadcasting station. In her June 11 OMS,[29] Berry reports that she was honored to introduce him for his WKY presentation and that he read "Oh Black and Unknown Bards" and "Go Down Death." Weldon died on June 26 when his car was hit by a train; Berry's eulogy for Johnson appeared in the *Negro Voices* anthology later that year. The poem is included in this collection.

Berry attended literary events such as Robert Frost's 1939 reading[30] at Central State University in Edmond, Oklahoma and Carl Sandburg's 1938 reading for the Oklahoma Educational Association, held in Oklahoma City.[31] She was also in the audience on May 19, 1938, when Mary McLeod Bethune spoke at Douglass High School.[32] In July 1938[33] and June 1939,[34] Josie attended the University of Oklahoma

---

[28] *The Black Dispatch*, "National Poetry Week," 10.

[29] "OMS," June 11, 1938.

[30] "Poet to Speak," 15.

[31] "OMS," February 12, 1938, 6.

[32] *The Black Dispatch*, "Douglass News," 6.

[33] *Sooner State Press*, "316 Persons Come to Writers' Course," 1–2.

[34] "OMS," July 8, 1939, 6.

Short Course in Professional Writing. She was likely the only Black person attending —in rolls of attendees, there are no other Black writers listed (that could be identified). She wasn't formally enrolled in the University—Black people were banned from admission—but in an extension course which did not fall under the university's segregation policy. The university couldn't deny her access to a state-funded public campus. OU didn't move toward desegregation until forced, in 1948, making Berry a campus-desegregation pioneer.

From October 29, 1937, to September 3, 1939, Berry wrote "Over My Shoulder," a weekly literary column for *The Black Dispatch*. Columns included reviews of a wide range of publications in several fields: science, poetry, economics, creative writing, nonfiction, and more. The column regularly included commentary on Black American life, information on Black and white literary developments, poems, and books by Oklahoma authors, black and white. In OMS for November 20th, 1937, under the heading "Ralph Ellison Goes Literary in *New Challenge*," she wrote

> Of particular interest to this column is the book review of *These Low Grounds*—W. E. Turpin by Ralph Ellison of Oklahoma City, now in New York. Good luck, Ralph.[35]

The breadth of Berry's reading practice as evidenced in OMS is astonishing. In her first column, she wrote that her reading schedule was "book-a-day, three-on-Sunday." She read books by nationally known authors as well as those by regional and local writers. As might be expected, she read deeply in Black literatures of all genres. She read and reviewed white authors as well. Perhaps defending herself from readers who complained about her inclusion of white writers, she wrote

> If you have read more than one OMS column you must have noticed that the space is not confined to Negro writers or characters. Our own contribution to America literature, either as writers or material for the

---

[35] "OMS," November 20, 1937, 6.

other group's pen, while of the utmost importance, is not the whole story by any means. Too many of our group are so blinded by the dust of the 70-year-old road we've travelled, they never glance at the parallel highways of other races reaching a thousand miles behind. We chant our plaintive spirituals or sing the weary blues so loud and long we do not hear the directions that will get us to the places toward which the others are heading. If we would just climb down off the worrying rock of blackness, half our troubles would be over. In these hectic times there are things far more important than skin hue that human beings should attend to at once. Black chauvinism and some historians to the contrary, notwithstanding, we do not hold all the firsts or lasts or onliests.[36]

Half of Berry's column that day was dedicated to a review of a novel by Welshman Wyn Griffith.

Berry subscribed to several magazines and newspapers, among them the *Saturday Evening Post, Saturday Review of Literature, Ladies Home Journal, The American Magazine, The Forum and Century, The American Mercury, The Negro Educational Outlook, The Crisis, Opportunity*, and *The New Challenge*. She also subscribed to regional literary publications such as *Kaleidograph, Southwester,* and *Arrow*.[37]

It would take several pages to list and describe all the book reviews published in Berry's columns. A selection of Black writers whose books she reviewed include W. E. B DuBois, Nick Aaron Ford, Zora Neale Hurston, Waters Edward Turpin, pioneer Black sociologist Bertram Wilbur Doyle, Arna Bontemps, Richard Wright, and agricultural economist Robert D. Brunson who was, at the time, a professor at Langston.

36 "OMS," January 15, 1938, 6.

37 These publications and the following authors were mentioned in OMS from 1937-1939.

Berry's shift toward leftist thought was first evidenced by her active participation in the Southwest Writers Congress. In her December 12, 1937, column,[38] she reviewed *The Writer in a Changing World*[39] which collected essays presented at the second national Writers' Congress in New York. She wrote mini-reviews of all sixteen essays in the book, most of which were authored by fellow travelers such as Eugene C. Holmes, a Black philosopher who taught at Howard University, Berry's friend and OU professor Benjamin Botkin, and Joseph Freeman, founding editor of both *The New Masses* and *Partisan Review*.

A 1956 *Black Dispatch* article reports that Berry had been named "local editor" for a page of Oklahoma City news in the storied Kansas City Black, newspaper, *The Call*, then edited by Lucile Bluford.[40] Given that *The Call* was known for articles about civil rights, school segregation, and urban development that devastated black communities, it seems sure that Josie remained a race woman, an honorific which Pauline Hopkins described in 1902:

> From the time that the first importation of Africans began to add comfort and wealth the existence of the New World Community, the Negro woman has been constantly proving the intellectual character of her race in unexpected directions; indeed, her success has been significant. From the foregoing we conclude that it the duty of the true race-woman to study and discuss all phases of the race question. (qtd. in Cooper)[41]

---

38 "OMS," December 25, 1937, 6.

39 Hart, *The Writer in a Changing World*.

40 "City News," 12.

41 Cooper, *Respectability*, 11.

Brittany C. Cooper, in the introduction to her book, *Beyond Respectability*, adds, "I choose to understand race women as public intellectuals."[42] Josie Craig Berry passed on Wednesday, February 4, 1981, at the age of 92. Surely her accomplishments, her lifelong dedication to her community, and her writings have earned Josie the title of public intellectual, of Race Woman.

The Poetry & The Text

The Collected Poems of Josie Craig Berry has been created in partnership with her descendants; without their support, this book would not exist.

The text comprises this introduction; a collection of Berry's publication bios and OMS entries about her life and her family's that serve as an "About the Author" entry; her collected poems; and an annotated bibliography for the poems. Annotations include relevant biographical, historical, and political information as well as line scansion and notes on her poetics. The 8 x 8 format of this book was chosen to preserve long-lined poems. Within each section, poems are ordered by date of publication, except for the last, post-1942 section where they are ordered by estimated dates of composition.

The first poem in this collection was written in 1918 when Berry was 29 years old. So far as research has determined, Berry did not publish poetry for the fourteen-year period between 1921 and 1936. Given her extensive prose and poetry publications from 1933-1940, one cannot assume that she wasn't writing. She was teaching, raising three daughters, and active in women's clubs. One wonders, too, if the 1918 death of her eight-year-old son, Henry Albert Berry, Jr., affected her desire to publish poetry.

Berry wrote poetry in received forms, in free verse, and in forms that she designed, often by combining or revising received forms. She often wrote accentual

---

42 Cooper, 15.

verse, that is, lines in which only strong accents—beats—are counted. Despite Berry's complex rhyme schemes, often combinatory, and the use of variable meter, the poems feel neither random nor overwrought. The poems cohere.

Berry's poetic influences range from Tennyson to Whitman to Frost. She wrote a subversive version of one Kipling poem and a humorous version of another. The King James Bible lays the ground for her insistence on civil rights and sings with Shakespeare in her iambic pentameter lines. She wrote an elegiac ode in heroic quatrains for Booker T. Washington and another in the same form for James Weldon Johnson. One poem reveals the rhythm and rhyme scheme of Browning's "Natural Magic."

Berry began to publish free verse in 1937. A free verse poem entitled "This Thing is Finished," won second place in a national poetry contest sponsored by the American Negro Exhibition (Chicago, 1940)[43]. First place went to Melvin B. Tolson who remains an essential Black poet.[44]

A 1970s notebook shared by Josie's descendants reveals that Berry was cataloging and ordering poems in preparation for a book. The final section of this collection, "After 1940," consists of previously unrecovered poems found in the notebook. In several of these later poems, Berry loosened her lines by moving away from accentual-syllabic lines to accentual lines. To many readers, accentual verse sounds like free verse, the ascendent structure of the time.

The poetry has not been edited for content and, therefore, Berry's use of the N-word in bitingly sarcastic poems remains. A few poems' structure has been edited; those poems were squeezed into narrow and short newspaper columns that made line and stanza breaks difficult to discern. In those cases, poetic form and rhyme schemes

---

43 *The New York Age,* "Negro Fair," 4.

44 Tolson lived in Texas at the time, teaching at Wiley University. In 1947, he began teaching at Berry's alma mater, Langston University, just up the road from Berry's Oklahoma City home.

have been utilized to set line and stanza breaks. Annotated bibliography entries for poems that have been corrected in this manner remark that they have been corrected. Obvious typographical errors in spelling have been corrected.

The Press plans to publish a collection of Berry's Over My Shoulder columns and other prose in the near future. It is the editor's hope that, through these publications, Josie Craig Berry will be recognized as an accomplished poet, a public intellectual, a literary powerhouse, and a woman whose contributions to Black literature and Oklahoma literature are immeasurable.

DO YOU WRITE POETRY?

If I should ever learn to write poetry, I'd be glad to pass on the rules, if there are any. I do know this much, pretty words and two words that sound alike used at the end of two lines of writing are not necessarily poetry. If you ever went to school and your fourth grade teacher asked you what the poem was about could you tell her? Usually a poem is written around one idea. If you have ten ideas that you must use in one piece maybe you had better write an article on sociology or religion or politics. And remember poems are usually cut by a pattern or mixed by a recipe. Did you ever see anything like your own verse? If you have something entirely new, better try some of the highbrow magazines. Do you know that "did go" and "did see," or "Thy and Thou," unless addressed to the Deity, are to modern poetry as bustles and high top shoes are to *Vogue* styles?

Who told you that you could write poetry anyway, or did you think it all up by yourself?

Why try to write poetry? There is certainly no money in it unless you are an Edgar Guess. Maybe you have the urge so strongly nothing will cure you. If so try to find out what it is all about. I'm reading or have read the following books on poetry that I can recommend to serious students:

Workers in Fire, Margery Mansfield—Advanced.
Introduction to Poetry, Alden—Beginners.
The Writing and Reading of Verse, C. E. Andrews—Beginners.
Conventions and Revolt in Poetry, Lowes—Advanced.
Enjoyment of Poetry, Max Eastman.

—Josie Craig Berry, OMS, May 14, 1938

Nota Bene

The poetry in this collection has not been edited for content.
It is published just as Berry wrote it.

Therefore, her use of the N-word
in bitingly sarcastic poems remains.

1918-1921

IN MEMORIAM
Henry Albert Berry, Jr. died May 3, 1918.

One year that seems but yesterday
Has passed since you, my son, hath crossed the Bar.
You stopped your earthly work and play
And pushed God's shining Heavenly Gates ajar.
We loved you, dear, in your short stay,
We miss you though you're near and yet so far.

The Family

NIGGER THIS, NIGGER THAT
Apologies to Mr. Rudyard Kipling

I went into a restaurant and sat down in a chair;
The waiter he up and says, "We serve no niggers here."
The people at the tables laughed and giggled fit to die;
I went into the street again and to myself, says I,
Oh, it's "Nigger this and nigger that," and "nigger, go away!"
But it's "Thank you, Mister Colored Man," when the band begins to play.
When the band begins to play, my boys, and bombs make night like day.
Then it's "Thank you, black American," when the band begins to play.

I went into a theatre as sober as could be;
They gave a drunken white man room, but hadn't none for me.
They sent me to the buzzard roost or else they sent me home,
But when it comes to fighting, Lord, they'll give me plenty room;
For it's "Nigger this and "nigger that," and 'nigger, wait out—side,"
But it's "Special trains for negroes" when the troopship's on the tide.
When the troopship's on the tide, my boys, and you clamber o'er the side,
Then it's "Special trains for negroes" when the troopship's on the tide.

Yes, making mock of faces that labor while you sleep
Is easy, and it's brutal, and it's also mighty cheap,
And struggling, trembling negroes to a tree or to a wall
Is ever so much safer than to face a cannon ball.
Then it's "Nigger this and nigger that," and "Niggers have no soul."
But it's "Strong black line of heroes" when the drums begin to roll.
When the drums begin to roll, my boys, and the Reaper takes his toll,
Then it's "Tried and true black heroes," when the drums begin to roll.

We aren't all black heroes and we aren't blackguards, too.
But simple human beings most remarkable like you;
And if sometimes our conduct isn't all your fancy paints,
Why negroes in the southland can't grow into plaster saints.
While it's "Nigger this and nigger that," and "Nigger, fall behind."
It is "Please walk in front, sir," when there's trouble in the wind.
We're the very first to fall, my boys, yet we leave our homes and kind,
For it's "Please to walk in front, sir," when there's trouble in the wind.

Some talk of better things for us, of school and work and all.
We'll wait for some advancement if you'll treat us rational.
Don't bother 'bout our morals so, but make the Stripes and Stars
To us an emblem of the free, and not of prison bars;
For it's "Nigger this and nigger that," and "Kill the burly brute."
Yet we black men saved you Teddy when the guns began to shoot;
And we've helped you all the long hard way from Concord to Carinal,
And we'll help you, Uncle Sam, against the Germans and them all.

We will do our bit for freedom's sake—your own, and ours, and home.
We will fight in muddy trenches or we'll brave the ocean's foam.
It's been "Nigger this and nigger that," and "Get on off the earth."
Yet, our own dear land of Dixie is the place that gave us birth;
Yes, we'll brave the common enemy on land, on sea, or sky;
If you'll only let us live in peace, we will show you how to die.

SONG OF THE NEGRO CLUB WOMEN
Sung to the tune of "America"

Humanity, thy tears,
Thy needs, thy wants, thy fears
   We'll strive to aid
Not as a meteor
But as a constant star
Whose light flames free and far
   Staunch, unafraid.

Always for right we stand,
Always a helping hand
   To those below,
Lifting as we climb
Eternity and time
Will show our faith sublime—
Onward we go.

Home of our faithful band,
Truly beautiful band,
   Thy needs we see;
Thy youth we'll help to save,
Help keep from felon's grave
Thy children whom God gave
   Fair Land, to thee.

Black race in thy distress
God in His righteousness
   Shall succor send.
Let us Light Bearers be
Throughout Eternity;
Lord we give praise to Thee.
   Amen! Amen!

AMERICANS AND AMERICANS

Oh, the Turk may kill Americans,
And the Greasers kill Americans
And the Germans kill Americans,
And there's trouble in the land!
If the Jap should catch and try them,
Or the Africa kill and fry them,
Or the Eskimo should buy them
——We would howl to beat the band.
But the redneck kills Americans,
And the poor peck kills Americans,
And the white trash kills Americans,
And they never do atone.
And the Dixons vilify them,
Vardaman says crucify them,
Blease lets Justice pass right by them—
Wilson sits quiet on his throne.

AND HERE'S TO YOU GOVERNOR EDWIN P. MORROW

Thanks to their just and righteous stand,
Kentucky hath not joined that other state
Where wild injustice and impassionate hate
Destroyed and disobeyed the law's command.

Of thee and Stanley in far distant years,
Kentucky's children will their children tell
How with undaunted courage but with tears,

The law is law for men both black and white.
And though so dark the criminal's disgrace.
Two awful wrongs will never make one right.
In justice's sun Kentucky takes her place.

THE FEMALE OF THE SPECIES
Apologies to Mr. Kipling

Harken all ye staid old bachelors
Who infest these crowded ways
You will likely be a victim
To this deadly leap year craze.
You had better get to cover,
Anywhere though it be jail,
For the female of the species
Is a gunning for the male.

Widows your days are numbered,
I expect the same advice
Would be good for you, tho scarcely
In your case will this suffice,
Once again the darts of cupid
Will your fortress-heart assail,
When the female of the species,
Goes a hunting for the male.

And she's a good shot too, I tell you,
When this old love game is played
Be she debutante or widow,
Divorcee or plain old maid.
Tho her heart may be a flutter
From her task she'll never quail,
When the female of the species
Goes a gunning for the male.

"SAVE"
A. Mitchell Palmer

They tell us to save up our dollars
Until they will buy for us more,
But prices of groceries and collars
Send creditor wolves to our door.

How can we save when we are starving?
How can we save when we are cold?
Expenses we've all been a-carving.
But money's to have, not to hold.

The rich man may save a few sheckles
But after he's paid up his tax,
And bought cream to lighten his freckles,
He'll tell you a few saving facts.

No matter how much we are making;
No matter how much we have made.
The present high prices are taking
It all, when everything's paid.

THE CHILDREN OF THE SUN

Tutt and Whitney took us traveling,
They were looking for the Light;
So they traveled in the day time,
And they journeyed in the night.

They went to far off Egypt,
And to flower decked Nippon,
They went to mystic India,
But they had to travel on.

They were harassed by the beggars,
They were lost in desert sands,
They were threatened by a swordsman
They were robbed by bold brigands.

But they kept right on a traveling,
Till they reached the Black Queen's home,
And they found the Light they sought for,
And no longer need to roam.

A Toast to the Leap Year Bride

Here's to you, Mrs. Jackson Barnett!
Long may you hold your name.
Here's hoping you will never regret.
You have tried the great love game.

If you can teach your beloved red man
To enjoy a bit of his wealth,
And if you will see that he travels around
And will take good care of his health.

Here's hoping you outwit the crafty ones
Who would take for their own, your gold.
You will earn your pay but you'll have your fun
Here's to you, what you Have you may Hold!

SPRING

Let mortals greet the glorious spring,
The green robed maiden whom all woo
Who comes along on fairies' wing
Or trips through showers and frost and dew.

The grim and hoary Father Snow
Recedes before her warming breath
And every where her footsteps go
She called back the world from death.

She brings the robin and his call
The shy wood violet lifts her head,
The tulips, daffodils and all
Appear in yellow, pink and red.

A rainbow of the fields we see
And joy shows forth in every thing,
Then hail fair maiden, hail to thee,
Thou resurrection symbol, spring.

WE'RE HERE

The immigrant is needed in his own home town,
and he's leaving U. S. or staying if he's there.
So the Yankee starts a holler and packs a big black frown
because he's set against it now, for fair.

He wants the foreign fellow to stop his hurried flight,
and stay and keep production up to par.
He really finds himself in a devil of a plight.
He sees ahead disaster not so far.

Now there's right here in America a flock of eager
hounds that reach for work that pays a living wage
and they're dyed-in-wool Americans, not scum from other lands
But their black skin shuts them in a doorless cage.

THE VICIOUS CIRCLE

The farmer blames the middle-man,
And HE blames the retailer,
And he in turn the farmer blames
While we starve and grow paler.
The sheep man blames the factories
And THEY the wholesale houses
And THEY say the department stores
Our black despair arouses.
It seems the wily profiteer
Has all his tracks well covered,
But soon we hope some daring sleuth
Will have his lair discovered!

WOE! WOE!

Woe, woe, unto thee, Georgia, land of death,
Thou art reeking with my race's precious blood.
Thou shalt some day cower there with 'bated breath
When Jehovah sends his retributing flood.

For every black man lynched, ten white men shall atone;
For every widow black, ten white shall be alone;
For every tear we've shed, you'll pay in blood and gold.
For every sin of ours, thine is a thousandfold!

The Land of the Free and the Home of the Brave that made the world safe for Democracy.

At Wacross, Ga., a white Southerner passing thru the Jim Crow section of a train threw a lighted cigarette into the lap of a colored woman; when her husband spoke in protest, he was shot to death and left at a station. No attempt was made to arrest the white murderer.
—The Crisis (1920)

A Prayer

From the time the fateful slave ship
touched the old Virginia Shore,
To the dim Mysterious future
stretching on forever more,

There descends upon our shoulders,
we, the women of this race,
Such a grievous, heavy burden
that but for Heaven's saving grace,

We'd be overwhelmed and foundered
for our efforts could but fail,
But with God to guide our vessel,
we will make a goodly sail.

We, untaught, untried, unlettered,
must our children teach and guide,
With our hands newly unfettered,
teach them Truth and Hope and Pride.

We must show the prowling white man
to his place and keep our own.
We must help the struggling black man
for we can't push on alone.

Great Jehovah in thy mercy,
thou didst to us Lincoln send,
Still we've unseen foes to conquer
and on Thee we still depend.

Help us, Father, on our journey
to Truth's ever beauteous light;
Let thy benediction hearten,
stay us with thy Love and Might.

Oft in voiceless supplication,
we thy tender love implore
Gracious Guardian of the Earthborn,
be our guide forevermore!

WHEN SUNDAY COMES ON SATURDAY

You've heard of divers miracles,
But this one beats them all.
For Sunday came on Saturday,
Which isn't right a-tall.

The Negroes need religion.
So Bill Sunday fixed the day,
When he would leave the white folk
And teach us Blacks to pray.

He knew that on the Sabbath,
He would save his good white folk.
So he told us that on Saturday
He'd adjust our Christian yoke.

Well, we didn't take the offer,
For we figured that Above,
This fellow has poor standing
With the Father, God of Love.

Christ taught that men are brothers.
This man calls us "you folk."
Now you'd not invite your brother
After the feast, that would be a joke.

And you wouldn't call him "You Folk"
And wonder if he had a soul;
So Billy Sunday we'll endeavor
Without your aid to reach the Goal.

We don't need your Tabernacle.
Nor your devilish Southern rule.
We'll jog on with our own Pilots.
While you still play "Religious Fool."

A PROPHECY

I don't know when the world will end.
I don't know when the stars will fall.
But I can predict a thing or two,
If I can't tell you all.
Wilson leaves the White House sure
Before another year.
And McAdoo, his noble son
Will not sit in his chair.
And there's a smile in old Ohio
On every single resident,
Because they know they're bound to give
Us, our next new president.

THANKSGIVING 1920

Oh East is East and, West is West and never the twain shall meet
Till earth and sky stand presently at God's great Judgment seat.
But there is neither East nor West, border, nor breed nor birth,
When two strong men stand face to face, tho they come from the ends of the earth.

Yes **Black** is **Black** and **White** is **White** and ever the twain shall part,
Till **Jesus Christ's Philosophy** shall dominate the heart.
But there is neither **Black** nor **White**, nor **Bond**, nor **Slave** nor **Free**,
When **Love** and **Justice** triumph **here** and guide **Humanity**.

And **Black** tho black, and **White**, tho white, and every **Kind** and **Race**,
Can meet upon one common ground, the long-sought **Council Place**.
And stature, habit, skin nor hair can make or mar a man,
When in his heart, the **Common Good and God's Law** take their stand.

We thank Thee, Lord, that **Black** is **Black** and too that **White** is **White**;
We love our **Race Integrity**: preserve it by Thy might.
Yet there is neither **Black** nor **White**, **Border**, nor **Breed**, nor **Birth**,
When **Real Men** meet life **Face to Face**, tho they come from the ends of the earth.

AN ODE TO WASHINGTON
Read at Recital of Portia Washington Pittman

Ah up from Slavery he came
To blaze the way to brighter things.
He did not flit on gilded wings,
But plodded to undying fame.

His was a heart whose every beat
Throbbed with the wish and the desire
To lift a slave race high and higher
'Till Lo! free men stood on their feet.

He was a man with vision clear,
Whose only aim was Service True,
Who had an humble thing to do
And labored for his race so dear.

He made the name Tuskegee, mean
A place where human hearts and hands
Are trained for Service, and all lands
of earth hold him in high esteem.

Long as the light comes from the sun,
Long as on earth achievements count
Long as shall stand the rugged mount
So long shall live our Washington.

An October Moon

Some may sing of silvery moon beams
Or of golden moon rise chant,
Some behold a cool pale lady,
Others coquette's eyes a slant;
But these beauties far surpassing,
Riding with a star platoon—
With its topaz fires rising—
Is the great October moon.

Lovers' moon struck in the glory
Of the Lunar beams alight.
Lip to lip they sense the story
That has kept the whole world bright.
Vows and pledges to each other
Are renewed, dawn comes too soon,
They could spend a lifetime sighing
Underneath October's moon.

Have you missed the mellow splendor
When the East begins to glow,
Never seen the red-gold fire
From the rim of orange flow?
A magician's power possessing
More potent than the rosy June,
See the love-light of the ages
Shining from October's moon!

LEST YOU FORGET

Uncovered heads and streaming eyes
Mark our last tribute to our dead.
We mourn for those brave souls who died
That Justice might her mantle spread.

And side by side the white and black
Americans pushed back the tide—
Columbia, we plead the cause
Of those black heroes who died.

Give their black mothers their rewards.
Let Peace at home discharge your debt;
Give their black babes a human's chance,
We ask again—Lest you forget!

UNTITLED

Twas only a face on a canvas
But the painter with mystic art
Put a look in the eyes of the maiden
That went straight to my lonely heart.
And I've traveled the whole world over
For a glimpse of that lovely face.
And I'll claim my own when I find her
In spite of her creed or her race.

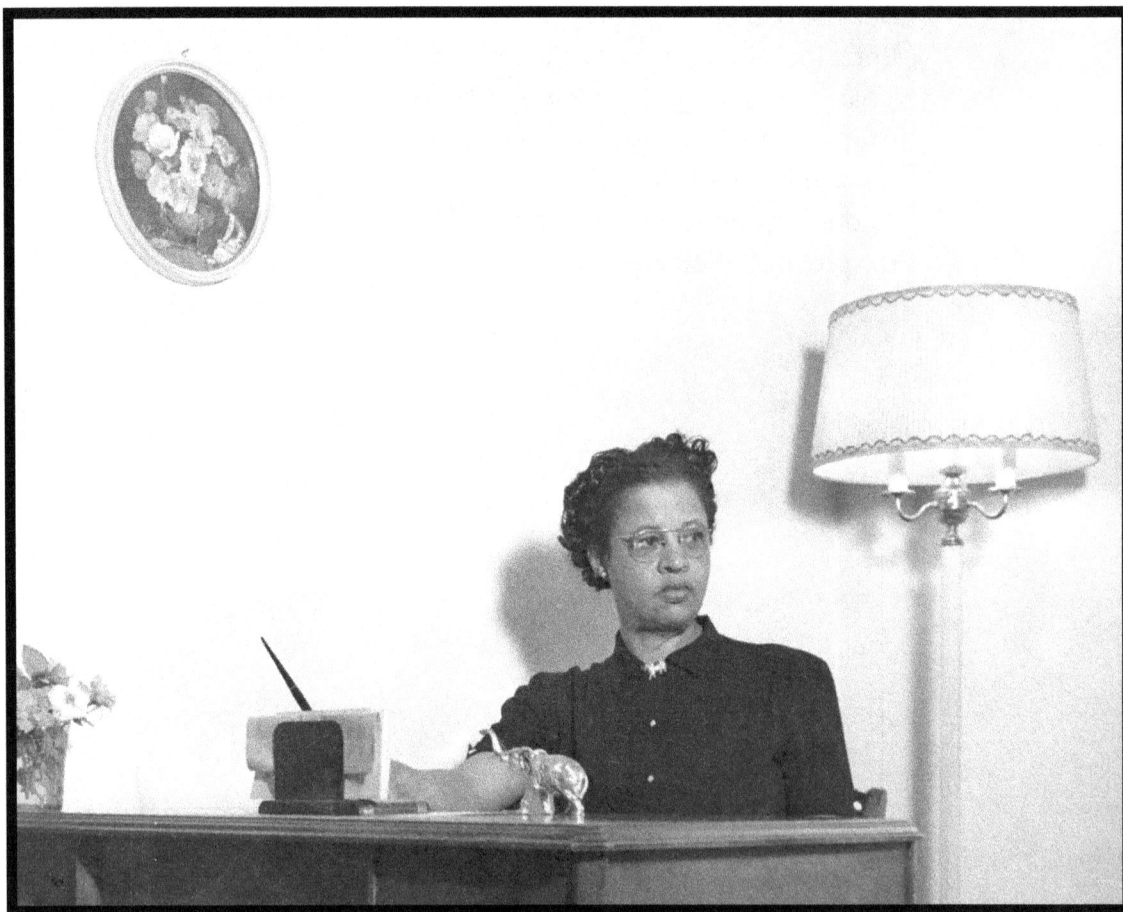

1933-1940

BOOKS (1933)

They are a goodly company
That sit around my board and at my fire.
With lovely Desdemona I commune at my desire.
I shudder at the vivid tales Poe pours into my ear,
I laugh and weep by turns, when Dickens doth appear.
I meet the gentle Jesus, as He was, when on the earth,
For Matthew tells the story of His mother and His birth.
I see the brave black soldiers defy the might of France.
With Cleopatra, queen of lover, and foolish Antony,
Hammurabi, the law-giver, explains the code to me.

So when some petty, low-brow modern slams his door in my face
Just because his thieving forebears stole the flower of my race,
I can laugh and spend a quarter for a book he cannot read,
A goodly company indeed!

FALL COMPLAINT

I live with coach and manager,
They argue all the time as to the chance
The pass has on a muddy field;
They plot how to advance
the ball, when outweighed fifteen pounds
Per man—life's not worth living
If this were not November
And the week before Thanksgiving.

DEATH TOWERS

The ceiling falls and racing neck and neck,
The plane and Death make for the landing field;
Your cruel fingers forged from steel and blood,
Clutch futilely, as wing to wing they speed
Death's filmy feathers, fashioned from the fog,
Fly out in fluttering beauty, just ahead–
The pilot shifts his course to miss your grasp
And pushes plane to safety and to life!

Then Death, outdone by inches, in a rage
Stabs out with vicious darts of blinding fire;
And since you failed to stop the freighted bird,
Death points the shafts at your up-rearing frame;
And cloud and earth and viscid cavern breath
Co-mingle in a deep and deadly roar.

THE DEVIL WRITES A LETTER
To the Senate on The Anti-Lynching Bill

Dear Editor: The Devil writes a letter
To the Senate on the anti-lynching bill;
His hot pen burns the paper, so he'd better
Let me the role, amanuensis, fill.

He says to tell the Senators who falter,
To sign this instrument to stop the mob,
And save both saint and sinner from the halter,
That they're the ones he needs now on his job.

He needs men who at heart dislikes a brother—
Imbued with fiendish glee or raging hate—
Can burn a man or see a baby smother;
He's waiting now for such at Hell's South gate.

He says to tell them that the world's opinion
Need not deter them from their brutal stand,
And that they'll have in his red-hot dominion
Much longer time to spend. Won't that be grand!

And so, Ed, print this note in red, like fire,
And have the extras shout both loud and well,
And sign it D. Beelzebub, Esquire,
Whose job is burning and whose address is Hell.

SANCTUARY

An eagle soared the blue immensity
Of awful heights to find a quiet place
To rear his eaglets; but in all that space
He found no spot of true tranquility.
Wars were upon the land-storms on the sea
These perils sinister he could not face
When 'neath his wing, the promise of his race
Lay steep—his bid for Immortality,

The isles were leveled by the hurricane,
The cities run by human beasts for prey;
The country isolation served in vain
To keep the dangers of the night away,
When home holds not a firm protective hand,
Will eagles find their rock in alien land?

OKLAHOMBI

Oh, red son of our prairies,
Do you not remember
That you alone, when circumstances called,
Forgot that you were mortal,
And with unwavering eye,
Defied grim Death?

Oh, prairie child of wind,
Oh, grandson of the moon,
Let not the perils of a peaceful time,
Snatch from your hand the token
Fame bestowed you.
Is it harder to be strong in peace
Than valiant in war?

WIND

The vicious swish of saplings warm to the west
That unleashed hounds of hell rush past the door;
They trample flat whatever man loves best,
The fledglings and the ancients fall before
The fatal flying feet. Ah! now they're gone—
But can, with course erratic, soon return.

BOOKS (1937)

They are a goodly company here at my board and at my fire,
All the wisdom of the ages visits at my heart's desire;
I weep with sweet Evangeline for love she found too late—
I hear the clicking needles driving Carton to his fate.

Winsome Portia pleads for Shylock, Hammurabi reads to me—
With Aeneas on his journey seeking what he knows not where—
Diving twenty thousand leagues with Verne; I go beneath the sea,
And then NORTH TO THE ORIENT with· Anne Lindbergh through the air.

Countee Cullen, Hughes and Dunbar, sweetest singers of their race,
Start the mellow notes revealing beauty in a dusky face.
I see the black ·black soldiers defy the might of France,
I watch the staid Egyptians in· their slow and stately, dance

Posturing for Cleopatra and her foolish Antony.
Slowly the Cid spreads splendor of old Aragon in Spain
And Kipling's singing soldiers start their slogging march again.
Magic books that keep the ages—plot the future for our need—
Master minds, ours for the taking—a goodly company indeed!

AWAKENING

The blossoming pear tree woke her eyes to love,
She hoped to see around her head a veil
As white and sweet—as poignant with the promise
Of life at last complete, as the petal shower around her.
Pear blossom and budding girl—Twin mysteries.

ENCROACHMENT

Dark Africa has crossed the dwindling seas;
She's tiptoed in to Nordic blood and manners
And now the kinky blond, in soft slurred
speech,
      "Detests the Niggers."

HERITAGE

      Thank God I'm black!
Dear Lord, since You have me endowed
With tropic streams of thick, rich jungle blood;
And since Dame Nature, Fate or You allowed
To thin this tide, a cold, pale, northern flood—
I'm thankful that the cooling, alien strain
Could not bleach out my sun-kissed Afric strain.

      Thank God I'm black!
I laugh while white kin weep and die,
My song stays with me; Lord, that's why
I fall to earth and rise a stronger soul.
I pity my white sister who bewails
The fact that she is partly black and fails
To sense the beauty of her heritage.

I'm nearer to the soil—yet near to Thee
I'm striving to ascend the heights—while she
Makes feeble effort to descend the depths
Of black despair—her white misery,
Her hopelessness is better left untold;
But when I write, I place at top of page
      Thank God I'm black!

THANKSGIVING 1937

I'm thankful that Man's Fall did not include
The grounding of my mind to sordid earth;
That in this span between my death and birth
My soaring spirit cannot be subdued.
When things mundane become too rough and rude
I'm free to change the bitter tears for mirth;
And though equators, measured, spell dust's girth
My soul springs past the mark—freedom imbued!

How dreadful if the body set the pace;
How limited the journey made by flesh;
But this does not obtain when awful space
Becomes by-paths where men their souls refresh.
I'm thankful, Lord, the body, not the mind,
Was grounded by the fall of frail mankind.

FALL HOUSEWIFE

Before the Winter puts the world to sleep,
Dame Autumn knits an afghan, warm and bright,
Of ravels of the summer and the spring,
To guard earth from the coming bitter night.
Chrysanthemums and dahlias—block by block—
With just a bit of green and lots of brown
She tucks in place—then waits for cloud and wind
To lay a spread of snowy crystal down.

HOME FOR CHRISTMAS
Thanks to Lloyd C .Douglas' book for title

To gay fires and warmth and laughter
From Florida to Nome
They're hurrying home for Christmas.
But what if there is no home?

IS THIS OUR WORLD?

Man sits complacently,
Cocksure and sound
The streptococci throw a chain
That mows him down.
Man strips the hillsides of the trees
And burns the wood;
Then water carries too much soil
For man's own good.

Man wastes the coal and oil—
Must have his fun;
He thinks the scientists will bring
Heat from the sun.
He shuts his probing eyes
To horrid waste;
Goes snatching at earth's savings bank
In frantic haste.

The Present, Now, at Once,
Not, After While;
Man may have shortened endless life
To one last mile.
He plows the spreading plain,
Turns under sod—
The dust storms snatch his livelihood,
And man blames God.

Man is the capstone to
Creation's day;
But of earth's creatures has
The briefest stay.
Man is a fool to think
He will endure.
He sits complacently, awhile
Sound and cocksure.

NINETEEN HUNDRED THIRTY-EIGHT

The page has turned—the turning
Has opened up long avenues of hope;
The Past is gone—no mourning
No bitter whimper, while we grope
For lost illusions
Will bring back one thing that's gone before
We listen to the closing of a door
On past confusions.

River Home

Once I thought that I would never leave the swirling, muddy river;
Once I swore that time for ever held me to the muddy shore;
But the prairies called and after farewells said twixt tears and laughter
I deserted barge and raft, I left them to return no more.

In the prairie winds I shiver, longing for my muddy river;
I should like once more to give her yellow length a full embrace.
But the prairie grasses hold me, I can not seem to unfold me
From the swift winds that cajole me to forget the river's pace.

So, although, I am still leery and am getting somewhat weary
Of these twisting winds contrary, that have laid this land to waste,
I shall never see the river—turning little—rushing ever
To the sea. My muddy river, decked with fringed palmetto's lace.

Life in Oklahoma

We must fight dust in Oklahoma if we make our homes worthwhile
For the dust storms and the locusts are encroaching mile by mile;
And the long droughts of the summer sear and wither earth and man,
The late frosts blast our orchards and upset our farming plan.
A forgotten, ancient legend damns our redbud on the hill,
And the marble halls of justice shake beneath the oil man's drill,
An unimpeded norther roars defiance in our face;
We just shake our heads and wonder who's the winner in this race.

A warm, deceptive winter seems like a Texas paradise,
And the foolish bulbs and flowers spend their Easter wrapped in ice.
Income tax is now so heavy we've lost a millionaire or two,
And the bureaucrats and paupers twist our heartstrings through and through;
But we'll fight with minds and dollars, hands and plans, this ought to help,
We're not leaving Oklahoma, though you still may hear a yelp.
This is home and we still like it, circumstances can't us lick;
Gosh! An April snow is coming; grab that shovel, come on, quick!

The Mother is a Friend Indeed
fragment from Josie's first printed poem

Though you wear the white rose
And I wear the red,
Your mother is living
Don't think of her dead.
She's moving and feeling
For her there's no night,
Though I wear the red rose
And you wear the white.

JUNETEENTH

The sudden severing of enslaving chains
Made overtones to shouts of men made free,
Who long had sung in sorrow sad refrains;
For June from New Year's seemed eternity.
At last to Texas on our southern shore
The message came to men already free;
And once again, though louder than before
The minor swell and burst in major key.

We've watched these seven decades come and go;
The sufferings of our race have lessened some—
The tread of Justice seems so stiff and slow—
We've stumbled often on the way we've come.
Ah, Lincoln, more than written word we need
To change the South and be free men indeed!

EL RENO EVENING

No sight like this can mountain dweller know;
His hills horizons build too high to see
The sun bends dazzlingly to kiss the wave
And leave a lip-stick print, so fleetingly
The sailor knows this miracle quite well
But he will not the ultimate attain
Until mid-continent sets stage for him
And western sun steps to the waiting plain.

AND DEATH WENT DOWN
To James Weldon Johnson

"Go down Death," the Master gave the word,
"Go down and fetch a singer from the throng;
"Bring back a voice that all the world has heard
"Bring back a man who sang a nation's song."

And Death went down; all heaven saw him go;
All heaven watched the beam for his return
Who was the chosen from the earth below,
For heaven's rejoicing, though the earth would mourn?

A black and well loved bard—though not unknown—
Who topped the heights that few men dare to climb,
Road back with Death—back to the Father's throne
On Death's pale horse, beyond the reach of Time.

FRUSTRATION

I've realized two life-ambitions,
I've had more real good breaks than most,
I've honored the family's traditions
But, so far, I can't make the *Post*.

These three wants of mine are pathetic,
The first had to do with a ghost,
The second, though peripatetic,
Is finished—the third—Make the Post.

I'd write villanelles to my own lips,
I'd drink to my own self a toast
If ever I thought, e'en for Post Scripts,
My blurbs would appear in The Post.

E. Jacobson, P. North and M. Fishback
Are heading the fortunate host;
If writer's cramp halts them, a poor hack
Like me, may, by grace, Make the Post.

LILITH-1937

What age did you say?
Why I'm younger than young—
Though I'm old as the moon
And saw seed from which sprung

Giant redwoods—and though
I'm old as the hills
I'm still younger than young,
I shall be found among

Those who view you when ills
Cause your dirge to be sung.
My face? It's my spirit
That's younger than young.

MODERNE
"American ballet stages filling station holdup."

Ballets and operas once held thrall
Because of grace and beauty.
But this passed, the hot-dog stand
Has pushed aside the castle grand,
And dames so proud and snooty
Have swapped their mantles for a shawl;
And cops cavort
Gas buggies snort
Where dancers once leaped now they crawl.

ONE ROYAL ROAD

It's bosh
To attend Harvard or Siwash.

The Indian, Sequoyah, with no education
Spent long weary hours with some bark and a stick
And finally got for the Cherokee Nation
A "paper that talked," quite a notable trick.

Wild Indians could learn it
Why should anyone spurn it?

He taught all who came to use the invention
In less than a week they had got a degree
But a sixteen-year struggle in schools make me mention
This language called English is still Greek to me.

Our college lawyer
Should copyright Sequoyah.

OUT ON THE PRAIRIE WIND, EASTERLY BLOWING

Out on the prairie wind, easterly blowing,
Half of New Mexico's no longer there,
Part of Nebraska rides with the terror—
The top of Dakota's in lanes of the air.

The tip of the panhandle, wind swept and broken,
Has left home for ever to settle elsewhere;
And cool Colorado, once Mecca of thousands,
Now comes thru the window, to thousands' despair.

The north part of Texas, once sodded with grasses,
Is down to a hard pan both sterile and bare;
And west Oklahoma, once an empire of barons,
Has taken the challenge and picked up the dare.

Out on the prairie wind, easterly blowing,
The dust bowl's huge crater's beginning to tear
At homes that were wrested from redman and bison
And a lone prairie grave all who've lived there shall share.

So Once Again, November

When Summer passed beyond the hills tonight
Hurried, yet held by Fall's reluctant chill,
I scanned the distance, waiting for this thrill.
So once again, November, the delight
Of your sweet season, time of pause and prayer,
Makes me forget the Winter's shortened day—
Lets me remember Spring's not far away—
Reminds my heart to mark another year.

WHERE ARE THE WARRING BRAVE?

Where are the warring brave of yesterday?
Where lie their rusting implements of pain?
Where are the banners, vanguards of the Way
That led them on into a lethal rain?
Was all their dying—all their hope in vain?
What is there now that's left to justify
Their sacrifice? What foothold did we gain?
What echo sounds the notes of their death cry?
What won a world that sent its youth to die,
Its best to fall, its noblest and its bold?
Have tears smoothed out the hummocks where they lie?
Will things be better when the world is old?

They did not know, not one courageous heart—
We'd circle on the trail to near their start.

SPRING AWAKENING

The poets wake, the poets rave
The poets muse and banners wave;
The elemental sap stirs in their veins
Which they turn into verse—
      (Help!)

Spring, Spring, oh beautiful Spring!
What joys and brightness do you bring?
I dance, I play, I shout, I sing
To welcome you. Oh beauteous Spring!
      (You would.)

The silent winter slowly draws its mantle.
      (Cause here is spring.)

In this that bit of glowing heavenly fire
That first our mothers warmed in ancient cave?
Whence came that glorious flash of crimson swiftness.
      (It's just a robin.)

The bare, stark limbs outlined against as dull a sky
Seem strangely stirred as if they fain would burst into
an instant greenness.
      (Sorry. Wind in a dead tree.)

Behold the melting softness of earth's flood of green
That yesterday was not and now—
        (That's chickweed.)

The melody I hear, can it be mortal?
Where learned the singer those ethereal strains?
I open wide my window wondering—
        (Close it again, you're tone-deaf, that's a sparrow.)

The peoples of the city throng to watch a sunrise,
And see enacted there the Play Supreme.
I rush to see if—
        (One Negro, Simon, got into one of these processions. You go home.)

TOWARD BETHLEHEM

The wakening north sped forth the messenger
Bearing soft skins, gifts of the hut and cave;
The smiling south, sun-kissed—mouth filled with music
Braved southern sands to cross and inland sea;
From out beyond the stretch of Samarkand
A racing camel bore spice and myrrh
In priceless alabaster, held in suave yellow hands;
The west lay dark and silent, waiting for that day
When they, too, would envision the Light
Whose Presence banished forever the deepening night
From all the hearts of men.

And thus a day was ushered in
By one great Star—
By Celestial chorusings
And shepherds praying on lone Judean hills.

Will north grow hostile and recall the bearer?
With south choke up with hurt and so forget to sing?
Will east replace the myrrh with hate and poison?
Will west remain too dulled to catch and retain the gleam?

The Star is there!
Oh, earthborn, are you blinded?
Where is your gift?
Your spice, your song?

To Robert Frost

You wish to know why sigh of leaves
And swish of boughs
About our dwelling place
Can never tire us:
Did our common mother forget to tell you
That when twin terrors-
The sudden pulsing scream of Sabretooth, or
The sickening fall
When tiny claws were loosed about her hairy neck,
Our last but ready refuge
Threw clutching branch to save us?
Were you never in the weary land
Where day's part-green shadows mock
And five-inch remnants of the dinosaurs
Roast on rocks?
Or sitting in the paths of icy and destroying gales
Were there no windbreaks to turn aside
The flattening wheels?
Did you not know that only trees
Prevent our continent from muddy suicide?
And though their restless talk of going
Belies the anchored roots' firm strength and sway.
Remember that the sounds of trees alone
Will let us catch and hold a wink of sleep.

OKLAHOMA CITY

On a lake called Overholser
Stands a city, Oklahoma;
All the sections of the country
Sent a score of sons to dwell there;
All the fair and far off cities
Sent their daughters to make beauty—
To make music with their voices—
To make homes that men and children
Would be cared for and contented,
In the new land vast and rolling,
In this west empire of promise,
In the land of Oklahoma.

And the men with stone and mortar
Built a fair and shining city,
Built a city for the future,
In the land of Oklahoma,
That would be to south and southwest
An example of endeavor—
Pattern of all civic progress.
And the women on the prairie
Planted redbud and petunia,
Planted maple, elm and poplar,

So their homes would be protected
From the burning sun of summer—
From the freezing cold of winter
Coming down from the Dakotas,
Sweeping down through Colorado.

Soon the streets and drives were leading
Out to parks and pools and playgrounds;
Soon the factories were humming,
Sending goods out to the farmlands;
Soon the prehistoric caverns
Gave their oil and gas to aid man.
All the tearful early struggles,
All the pains and disappointments,
Time has softened for the city;
And she stands on Overholser,
Fair, and each day growing fairer.
Rich, and each month growing richer,
Good, and each year growing better—
Southwest's queenly Oklahoma!

THIS THING IS FINISHED

When we near the end of time
There will be wars still fomenting and unfought;
There will be squalid huts
Where pallid wraiths in human form
Spew forth their young, to eat, to propagate, to die.
There will be greed that lesser men
Will use to batter better men than they
Back into the primordial mud from which they came.

Those things go on until the end of time:
Antipathies of race and creed;
Blood hate of brother for a brother's blood,
And the slicing rapier of a sister's tongue that slays a sister;
The maniacal cunning of a devil's master mind
Housed in the image of a god called man;
The trusting ones who only live
To be made fools of by the clever fools
No cleverer than they.

Some things are done before the end of time.
There was the sunset where the giant disk
Stood flush with the prairie's edge like a dollar on a table;
There was the heaped-up blue of Michigan
That rose into a gradual hill
Against a matching sky;

There swayed the green-robed choir with deep cream faces,
Who sighed beneath a southern summer sun.
And sifted on a sudden summer breeze
A scent we call magnolia:
There was the tender pulsing of a feathered flute and viol
Close to dawn;
There was the day so choked with dust
Breathing became a measured race with Death,
The wind setting the pace and holding stakes-
The sun a queer electric blue that cut the murk
And bade us hold the pace
With promise of tomorrow;
There was glory in a thunderhead
That tore our souls asunder
With the beauty of a changing mauve and gray.
We treasure up these finished things
To stay us till the certain end of time.

I Am Not Done with Love

I am not done with love because you left
So large a debt of tenderness unpaid.
I face anew my life and unafraid
Pick up the threads. I shall with fingers deft

Weave ageless dreams of moonlight, song, and you—
Of words you spoke while yet our love was young—
Of looks too eloquent to need tongue.
I am not done with love because you threw

The splinters of my heart into the fire
Of your forgetfulness, and left me cold
And shivering in your state of lost desire.
Although your heart to mine I could not hold

The memories you left can never die.
You may done with love, but never I!

I AM NOT DONE WITH LIGHT

I am not done with light because the tears
Oft blasted have curtained fast my sight
And stretching out into an endless night
Roll the dark vistas of my wasted years
My faltering footsteps and my shadowed fears
Black out at times that vital inner light
Without which man's whole urge becomes a plight
That stifles all his ardent soul reveres.

I am not done with Light because my eyes
Cannot behold the task so late begun
Though trivial things my sightlessness denies
Beyond the dark shines an eternal sun.
The thundering echo of an end implies
There is away to go—a race to run.

AREOPAGITICA

Dare we speak out?
It seems that if these ills are ever cured
Some one must speak,
and speak so he is heard.

We've hidden cankers that eat up the soul:
We've covered sores that braver lands
Have bared to sun and air
and prayed aseptic peace.

The lilac-scented spinster of the ease,
The bigot in the black ecclesiastic robe,
The narrow-minded drudge whose only spree
Rocks her in holy drunken ecstasy:

These and some others do not wish to see
The sadists' funeral fire deep in the south;
They try to feed the ill-spawned hungry brood
Of men whose flesh had better been left clay,
Who care not if today they eat
And if tomorrow earth is turned to dust.

So some of us must speak, and speak so loud
That timorous tirades are drowned at birth;
That opposition to the spread of truth
Will strangle in our righteous thunderings!

What Do They Know?

That cop nearly got me that time. I must be more careful. Gosh, how I'd like a drink of water! Those cigarettes are life savers. Now that's a laugh. Life savers! I, who am about to die! You'd think that the crowd was crazy instead of me—a fool human fly, perched just high enough to turn these arms to wings and get me out of a devilish mess as easily as the sparrows swoop down to the pavement! Lord, that pavement looks a long way off and as solid as the earth itself. Wonder how far I'll fall before I black out? Maybe I won't have to go after all. Been up here since six o'clock and the sun is getting low. Bud must be as jittery as I was before I decided to take this way out in case—

Crowd is getting bigger. "What fools these mortals be" just half describes them. Gosh! I have picked a messy path to Glory. Glory? Small chance there will be much glory for the family if Bud doesn't get the breaks. He's a pretty smooth fellow but this is the toughest spot a Jones boy has got himself into.

Well, now, that's a queer contraption. They sure want to save mopping up that sidewalk. Sorry, but up here I have all the time to give Bud a chance and at the same time get ready to do my good deed for today—and a good deed it is if it has to be. Queer how a long clear road suddenly develops corners and bad turns. Thanks, the last pack was about gone. Sure, I have a match. Go chase yourself, this is my party. Oh, smart guy, eh? Well, come on out and there will be two covered splashes —and it's a long way down. I should know as I have had plenty of time to figure it out. Get to hell about your own business.

Lord! That looks like Bud. It is! Things are getting dark. I'm afraid to look at the signal. It is sure a long way down. I'll get no medal for this but when I step off, I'll pin one on myself. No point in gazing skyward now. Bud's down there and he has the answer. Well, here goes. Gosh, he made it! Good old Bud! Safe! Lord, what a narrow ledge! I'm getting dizzy. Oh, God let me reach the window! I'm afraid to move. It's such a long way down.

THE BALLAD OF BILL MALONE

1918
Bill Malone was a lazy scamp,
He was hardly more than a ragged tramp;
He wasn't worth a cancelled stamp
    Before the war.

His wife scraped the wherewithal
To hush her hungry children's call;
but Bill, he wouldn't work at all
    Before the war.

They looked him over and he was sound,
But you'd never see for miles around
A fellow that looked more out and down
    Before the war.

Well, of course he'd never go enlist
But they drafted him by fate's strange twist
And he said "I'll go if you insist,
    To win this war."

For he stumbled along with a forward slump,
And he couldn't hop or skip or jump,
And he mostly leaned against a stump,
    Before the war.

When his wife went down to see him off
Says she to Bill, "Now mind your cough,
When you were here you had it soft,
    Before the war.

"If you can't stand it, write to me
And I'll alarm this whole country,
I'll go to Washington and see
    About this war!"

When he got to camp the sergeant sighed,
"Here's another had eggs to be fried;
I know he's punk before he's tried
    To learn this war."

So they confiscated Bill's old flask
And set him at a trenching task;
Bill turned to his bunkie then and asks,
    "Hell, is this war?"

"When I learn how and get over there,
I bet I make the Kaiser swear;
I'll take his scalp or gray his hair,
    About this war."

Well, the whole battalion picked on Bill;
They made him work and they made him drill
Till I thought the poor fish would be ill
    Before the war.

But he straightened up and he drilled away
And soon was drawing a corporal's pay;
And he grinned and said, "Now come what may,
　　I'm in this war."

He sent his money to his wife,
And he says to her, "Go enjoy life,
This here ain't such strenuous strife,
　　This here big war."

Well it turned out just like old Bill said,
He got over there and charged ahead
And bombed 'bout a hundred Boches dead
　　In his first war!

As he didn't get back we thought he's lost,
But late that night someone says, "Ole Hoss,
The captain says I'll get a brass cross
　　After the war!"

1939
Now Bill's young son when stops to heed
And ponder the depths of his country's need
Remembers that he and his pa agreed
　　Concerning war.

That a scrap in Europe is a hell of a plan
To get democracy for a colored man;
But the lad will probably do all he can
　　In this next war.

JUNE

When the sky is blue
And the air is clean,
When the flowers bloom
And the grass is green,
When fires spring up
In cheek and heart,
Who could keep lovers far apart?

PEACE

A new commandment give I unto you that ye love one another. John 13:34.

"Peace! Peace," they cry and there can be no peace
And bloody Mars' most frightful tempers rage;
The nation's death in flaming fire release,
And men in dreadful orgies now engage.

"Peace! Peace," they cry and there can be no peace
Until the earth is swept of rankling ire;
And men and nations must their wailings cease
And bravely, pass right through the purging fire.

"Peace! Peace," they cry but why should there be peace
Until the world is rid of hating men;
Until from poverty there is surcease,
And rank oppression rushes to its end?

"Peace! Peace," they cry and yet, there will be peace
When men as brothers travel hand in hand,
And justice, truth and right and love increase
And nations heed the Blessed Christ's command.

AREOPAGITICA

Dare we speak out?
It seems that if these ills are ever cured
Some one must speak,
and speak so he is heard.

We've hidden cankers that eat up the soul:
We've covered sores that braver lands
Have bared to sun and air
and prayed aseptic peace.

The lilac-scented spinster of the ease,
The bigot in the black ecclesiastic robe,
The narrow-minded drudge whose only spree
Rocks her in holy drunken ecstasy:

These and some others do not wish to see
The sadists' funeral fire deep in the south;
They try to feed the ill-spawned hungry brood
Of men whose flesh had better been left clay,
Who care not if today they eat
And if tomorrow earth is turned to dust.

So some of us must speak, and speak so loud
That timorous tirades are drowned at birth;
That opposition to the spread of truth
Will strangle in our righteous thunderings!

AFTER 1940

About This Section

A 1970s notebook shared by Josie's descendants reveals that Berry was cataloging and ordering poems in preparation for a book. This section, "After 1940," consists of previously unrecovered poems found in the notebook.

The tables of contents in the journal listed sixty-one poems. The list does not include all the poems from the first and second sections of this collection. Thirteen poems on her list were published and previously recovered. Seventeen poems, handwritten in her notebook, are previously unrecovered poems. This section consists of fifteen handwritten poems from the notebook. Two of the hand-written poems are incomplete—they are not included in this section.

An earlier, previously-unrecovered, poem—"I Am Not Done With Love," is hand copied into the journal. In a 1939 column, Berry refers to a "trilogy" of sonnets and states that "I Am Not Done With Love," which is printed in the column, is a part of the trilogy. In her notebook, Josie enters all three titles, "I Am Not Done With Love," (published in 1939), "I Am Not Done with Light," and "I Am Not Done with Life." The third poem of the trilogy, "I Am Not Done With Life," remains unrecovered. "I Am Not Done With Light" is placed in the 1937-1939 section with its sister-poem.

Berry enters into her notebook titles of another trilogy, "The Kennedys." Two were hand-copied into the journal: "The Dark Came Swiftly (for JFK)" and "I Have No Tears To Shed (for RFK)." The third, "A Task Remains," written for Ethel Kennedy, was not in the notebook and remains unrecovered.

Berry listed two poems for Dr. Martin Luther King. The first, "I Have Not Marched" appears to be written before his assassination—it's a pledge to join the marches. The second, "Who Leads the March Today?" was likely written after his death and remains unrecovered. Also in the notebook are six lines of a poem about the 1968 Orangeburg police massacre of young Blacks who were holding a peaceful protest against a racist act. The poem is incomplete, so it is not included.

Most of the poems in this section were written after 1969. A few years after the death of her husband in 1965, Berry moved to California to live her daughter, Allison. Berry's poetry expanded to include California topics: wildfires, giant redwoods, and Lawrence Welk's music.

The excitement of recovering the poems in Josie's notebook is tinged with grief for the poems now lost, perhaps forever.

PRAY FOR MIDNIGHT

No moon disturbs the lush
rare dark of this rare rare night
No bird stirring, no fox hunting
Nothing breaks the blessed silence.
Only once perhaps will come
this hour to many men.
So Pray for midnight.

Oh, God, delay the light
that shows a brother different.
Let me this one grand moment
Feel with my heart his humanness
Awake someone within.

THE DARK CAME SWIFTLY
for John Fitzgerald Kennedy

A sun has set,
the dark came swiftly
Hiding a river of tears
of an anguished nation.
A heart-leak of inconsolable grief
Eyes opened wide in startled disbelief.
A sun has set and stars forget to shine.

I HAVE NO TEARS TO SHED
for Robert F. Kennedy

I have no tears to shed,
the font is dry.
The weathered hopes all
but stifle the days ahead.

No! No! Not again, Dear God.

Fate schemes to add to an
already back-breaking load
To test the mettle of a super clan
Only this morning he was so alive.

He can't be dead!

That early setting sun—
This unbelievable disaster—
Well-lighted every shock
And again a bright young master.

I HAVE NOT MARCHED
to Martin Luther King

I have not marched nor raised my voice in song pentameter
I may have flinched but never fled before approaching wrong.

This is the way I am— the way I was meant to be
From birth to walk through hell to reach eternity.

Let both equator and the distant poles
Become a battlefield when I must go.

And go I will but not with clapping hands to shield
me from the searing sun torch of a taunting foe.

DWINDLING HOPES

If what I feel is any indication
If what I hear and see is
happening beyond all control.
Much that I see and hear
leaves me unmoved,
The heart I had has lost all
connection with pulse of pride
with dwindling hopes
of a lost tomorrow.

I Saw a Giant Fall

All through the years of centuries it stood
A tower for the weaklings and the timid to look upon;
To take heart and use the promised six score and ten
To root a monument to bolster the hopes of men.

But the devil's teeth of saws could not contain
Their greedy munching of this precious spire
And now on long smooth banks soon to
become the aftermath of wind and fire.

And nature starts a seed to grow
A thousand years or more—again.

FIRE ON THE MOUNTAIN

The wind, blowing westward
Look at the birds
Louder and louder
than any I've heard

The sun seems to travel
Riding high in a haze
The sun's getting heavy
Oh, God, there's the blaze.

To the top of the Badlands
Skirting acres of grain
Up up on the rocks
Where the chaparral grows
without snowflakes or rain

Seven hundred—maybe more
flee for their lives.
The red wagons arrive.

THANKSGIVING 1970

Thanks for the music
That bubbles like wine
With melodic dancing
Like the winds in a pine

Thanks for the cadence
That still lingers on
In the hearts of the listeners
When the singer is gone.

When We Greet the New Year

When we greet the New Year
What gifts shall we bring?
A golden tiara—
a big diamond ring?

Sweet words of comfort
A friend's heartfelt tear?
A smile of forgiveness
To grace the New Year.

How shall we be using
Each precious day?
There will be the same hours
springing blithely away.

We must use them or lose them.
These will not come again.
If the minutes are treasured
A wealth of memories remain.

ADVENTURER

He climbed the mountain
Threatening and steep.
He rode the rapids leaping
high and deep.
The snow, the river, the
approaching rain
Made him resolve just one more
time again.
But to the city on a
freeway hill
He braced himself for one more
racing thrill.
He pushed the throttle just a
mite too far
Then took the certain highway to a
distant star.

OLD TERRA FIRMA

Jonah rode in comfort in the
belly of the whale
But my frantic heart beats faintly
In this fierce Pacific gale

The big tin bird keeps going
Going but not knowing where
The pilot pulling saddle
on his bouncing bucket chair

I cling to old terra firma
while this ballet ponders sleet.
Just a glimpse of earth not heaven
would be plenty and complete.

WHERE ARE THE CHILDREN?

I saw a marker on an island hillside
just a stone's throw away from Pearl Harbor.
A simple stone among the thousands that
stretched to the edge of our beginning.
Chips of an eternal flame.

Small and lonesome on a Kansas prairie .
And others scattered near an inland sea.
They may be planted in a plot up Boston Way
where Britain's sons and our own young men
now have no answer, neither where or when.

THE WINDS OF CHANCE

The winds of chance are
blowing blowing blowing
And on this rock
I wander all alone

The questing tides keep
flowing, flowing, flowing
toward distant lands
but none I call my own

Oh winds of chance
send me a sail, a token
Maybe a voice like
I remember spoken
to calm my fear
and to strive live

This day, help me through.

PRAYER FOR 1975

I thank thee, Father life—
A rendezvous with Death, you say?

Clutch to your heart the songs the
angels sang long before your trip here.
Back to the eternal happiness of peace.
And love of glory from the distant
spheres of unlimited enchantment,
the glimpse of light
that becomes now and forever.

from The Black Dispatch, January 2, 1920
Mrs. Josie Craig Berry. The brilliant young woman who has so many times inspired our readers with her classic gems of poetry. Mrs. Berry is one of Oklahoma City's former school teachers. She is prepared in every way, both in her evenly balanced temperament and culture, to give the reader of *The Black Dispatch* food for thought that rhymes. One of Mrs. Berry's best poems and one that sticks so hard by truth is the one entitled "Nigger This, Nigger That."

from Southwester Anthology, January 1937
Josie Craig Berry (Mrs. H. A.) lives in Oklahoma City, Oklahoma. Mrs. Berry was educated in public and private schools, finishing at Harvard. For some years she taught science in the Oklahoma City Schools. Her family consists of three daughters and her husband. Mrs. Berry's verse has been published in many newspapers and magazines. She is a sponsor and member of the Oklahoma Poetry Society, associate member of the Southwest Writers' Congress and holds the presidency of Semper Fidelis and Little Playhouse clubs. She has been a member of the Shakespeare club for twenty-five years.

Written by Josie, in Over My Shoulder, The Black Dispatch, May 21, 1938
When Dean Hardy Liston of Knoxville college, visited Oklahoma recently he was struck with the wealth of material for writers of both fiction and fact. I opened the April *American* and "Cotton and Clayton" met my eye. Cotton and Clayton! How familiar they sounded.

It seemed Beverly Smith visited in England during the 1920's. His Liverpool acquaintances wanted to know about Mr. William Clayton. The American had to come home to find out just who William Clayton was. The article, "King Cotton Himself," explains what he found.

But back to Oklahoma, Before I reached it in the story something clicked and Anderson and Clayton of Oklahoma City identified King Cotton.

My father worked for the silent partner of the old Harriss-Irby Cotton Company for over forty years. William Wallace Bierce was a power in more than one southern business concern. The two cotton firms were on friendly relations though each was the other's most powerful competitor.

The romance of cotton is interwoven all through my childhood. Should I ever get my book together I have the two prerequisites of a Negro writer. My mother was a washerwoman at one time. She ran a shirt laundry and cleared fifteen dollars a week for herself, which was more than most men made at that time; and I picked cotton, even though it was less than a hundred pounds for the one week I persuaded my mother to let me go with a schoolmate to her father's farm at the edge of the little town. All I need now is the manuscript.

At Memphis I have seen the specially constructed steamboats loaded with the bales which were piled on the outside and heard the roustabouts swing their rhythmic chants. In Mississippi I saw tall cotton stalks that a child could climb. In Chalmette, which was started by the Bierce crew of which my father was ·the only Negro, I saw cotton pressed and loaded for foreign markets; later from this suburb to New Orleans only two miles away, I saw the floats in the Mardi Gras glorifying the white-gold fleece, and then in Oklahoma where the small-stalked cotton yields a much longer staple than the rank growth of the south, I saw my father at his work as sampler, where, with a short, broad-bladed knife, he could slash through the tough jute sacking with one stroke and take out the double handful of staple to the tune of five hundred bales a day.

Yet with material all around us here in Oklahoma someone must hear of a man in England in 1920 and come home to write him up in 1938 and introduce us to someone and something we have known all our lives.

Mr. Clayton is still connected with the Anderson-Clayton Cotton Company of Oklahoma City. He has not lived in Oklahoma City since 1918, but calls Houston, Texas, home.

from Over My Shoulder, The Black Dispatch, July 29, 1939, page 6
Dear Readers:

Sorry we were so busy getting educated last week that we missed getting our copy on time.

We were part of the summer class of '39 along with our former pupils, Goldie Norman, Agnes Ellison, H. L. Parker, Fred Davis, Elmira Richardson Todd and Madgee Brewer Sneed.

A very dignified young man in a mater's hood and gown presented our group, the Bachelor of Science in Secondary Education to the president for our degrees. He was another pupil of ours, Hilliard Alphonso Bowen, now a professor of education at Langston University.

Two other young profs, Jack Jefferson and Wyatt Slaughter of the chemistry department extended best wishes to their former general science teacher. So you see, I was a busy and happy person.

My mother, Mrs. Josie Craig and my husband, H. A. Berry left Oklahoma City to witness my graduation. They both came to Knoxville College on a similar occasion quite a long time ago. My youngest hopeful, Alison, drove over from Okmulgee to take her dad and me to the baccalaureate sermon Sunday, July 16, which was preached by our old friend, Rev. A. M. Johnson of Calvary Baptist Church, Oklahoma City.

Josephine Berry Lane, the second daughter, was there to help me don the cap and gown. We are the two odd members of the Berry tribe having B.S. degrees with biology and science majors while the others, H. A. and Erycina Berry Hoskins of Shelby, North Carolina, are A.B.'s with language majors and Bill, the baby or as she now prefers to be called, Miss Helen Alison Berry, has an A.B. with sociology major and a two year professional certificate from the Atlanta School of Social Work.

Dad and the kids have their degrees from Knoxville College.

Bennie and Zenobia Taylor brought my folks over to the exercises. The Taylors had four cousins in the line of 110 graduates. Quite a nice thing when more than one branch of a family is trying to get ahead.

The honorable Dr. Byron K. Armstrong delivered the address and our own beloved president, Dr. J. W. Sanford, welcomed us into the ranks of the educated.

Which reminds me that Plato and Aristotle may have been able to encompass the world of knowledge in their time but it is beyond the power of any of us to get more than a glimpse of a single branch of our social heritage of today.

We have come a long way through a path starting at LeMoyne Institute, a New Orleans Convent, public schools in Mississippi, Mary Holmes Seminary at West Point, Miss., Knoxville College, summer session at Harvard University, extension courses taught by O. U. and Oklahoma City U. instructors, and ending for the time being at Langston.

It has been a pleasant journey and we are humble and grateful that we have had the privilege of passing this way.   —J. C. B.

from Negro Voices: An Anthology of Contemporary Verse, August 1939
Josie Craig Berry (Oklahoma City) attended a New Orleans convent, Knoxville College, Harvard and Langston Universities, and was a teacher of science in Oklahoma City for eleven years. She is married and has three daughters, but finds time to take a final course in sociology at Langston, edit a newspaper column, review books for two papers, and write verse which has appeared in several magazines and anthologies. Mrs. Berry introduced James Weldon Johnson when he read two of his poems over an Oklahoma radio station during Poetry Week this year It was shortly after that that Mr. Johnson met his tragic death and Mrs. Berry dedicated her poem to him.

from Ogden Standard-Examiner, October 23, 1942
At the close the building, of large proportions, equipped with many conveniences, was turned over to Mrs. Josie Craig Berry, as USO center director. She is an educator from the schools of Oklahoma City, where she has been a science teacher. She knows her own people and therefore is capable of leading them. She has won a number of national honors in poetry and comes highly recommended.

THE PHOTOGRAPHS

All photos courtesy of the family—dates and locations are approximate.

Before Introduction: Henry Albert Berry and Josie Craig wedding, June 1, 1909

Page 1: Knoxville College Graduation, 1908

Page 16: Douglass High School Teacher Photo, 1930

Page 29: Josie at Her Desk (Writing OMS?), 1937

Page 68: Hampton University Staff Photo, 1941

Page 81: Josie and her Grandson, Crawford Henry Lydle III, 1954

Page 97: Henry & Josie's 50th Anniversary, 1959
Adults, left to right: Josie Craig, Erycina, Alison, Henry, Josie, Josephine

The family prefers not to name the children.

Berry, Josie Craig. "A Fall Complaint." *The Black Dispatch,* October 20, 1933.

    This poem is best described as a "ditty" lamenting the deleterious affect that Oklahoma's football madness has taken on the Berry household. Henry Berry was the first coach of Douglass School's football team (1908); the "manager" is likely Henry's best friend, Lucius McGee who, along with F.T. "Frenchy" Bruner, assisted Coach Berry ("Douglass High School"). Recovered 2022.

———. "A Prayer." *The Black Dispatch*, September 3, 1920. Oklahoma Digital Newspaper Program. The Gateway to Oklahoma History, https://gateway.okhistory.org/.

    Eight iambic tetrameter quatrains (long measure) rhyming ABCB. A Prayer that God will become the Guardian of Black people. Berry starts with a remembrance of slave ships, comments slavery's damage to black people, Recognizes that God "didst to us Lincoln send / Still we've unseen foes to conquer and / on Thee will still depend."

———. "A Prophecy." *The Black Dispatch*, July 9, 1920. Oklahoma Digital Newspaper Program. The Gateway to Oklahoma History, https://gateway.okhistory.org/.

    Written as amphigory (nonsense) verse. Three quatrains, 4/4/4/3 beats to lines. It can be recited to the rhythm of "Jabberwocky." The poem is a "political prophecy" that Wilson will lose, and that "there's a smile in old Ohio / On every single resident, / Because they know they're bound to give us, our next new president." Harding, who won the election, has been historically evaluated as being sensitive to issues concerning women and minorities ("Wilson").

———. "A Toast to the Leap-Year Bride." *The Black Dispatch*, March 19, 1920. Oklahoma Digital Newspaper Program. The Gateway to Oklahoma History, https://gateway.okhistory.org/.

    Written in song measure (podics 4/3/4/3), rhyming ABAB. Oklahoman Jackson Barnett, a Creek / Muskogee, was known as "the richest Indian in the world," due to oil royalties from his allotment. This poem, dripping with sarcasm, speaks to Anna Laura Lowe, a known "fortune hunter" She married Barnett, then in his 70s, thereby gaining control over half of his fortune, the other half going to Bacone Indian College. Anna promptly moved them to a Los Angeles mansion where Barnett died in 1934 ("Barnett").

———. "Adventurer." *Personal Notebook*, n.d., Circa 1974

    Poem of four undivided quatrains rhymed ABCB. The poem is a fair yet humorous representation of the great male adventurer featured on 1970s television news and sports coverage.

————. "Americans and Americans." *The Black Dispatch*, February 7, 1920. Oklahoma Digital Newspaper Program. The Gateway to Oklahoma History, https://gateway.okhistory.org/.

Two octaves of tail rhyme (AAABCCCB). B-lines of two beats; all others, three. Because the poem was squeezed into a short and narrow newspaper column, the lines and stanza breaks were determined by the rhyme and form. A justifiably harsh poem criticizing Wilson for intervening in WWI while not intervening in American racial violence. Black Americans are killed by the "redneck" the "poor peck," and the "white trash." Meanwhile, "Wilson sits quiet on his throne." Berry calls out, by name, the "Vardaman," and "Blease" who were Jim Crow southern politicians. She also names "the Dixons," a "mulatto" father and son who found the dead body of a young white woman and were assumed to have killed her. The uproar over the incident is believed to have led directly to the lynching of John Carter who was assumed to have been responsible for the disappearance of two white children ("Vardaman," "Blease," "Carter").

————. "An October Moon." *The Black Dispatch*. October 20, 1921. The Gateway to Oklahoma History, https://gateway.okhistory.org/.

Three octaves of three-beat lines rhymed ABCBABCB. The first version of the poem, "An October Moon," was published 20 October 1921 (p. 5, in *The Black Dispatch*. The *Southwester Anthology* version (1937, 64), which had two slight revisions, will be used in this project. *Southwester* version republished in OMS on 15 October 1938, with the following note: "When my favorite verse was printed last fall, I did not use it in OMS but remarked that the column might be short when October came around again. Today I am in a maze of the viscera of the dogfish shark. Wm. Ogburn's report on the family in the Hoover investigation of recent social trends, a weekly precise of The New York Times, editorials, wondering if Culture had any origins and dodging my French teacher who insists on conversational French. So it was with startled delight that I greeted the waxing, 'Harvest Moon.' This is the lovers' moon. Watch for it as she comes up the evening of the full moon, shedding its light on the synchronized hearts of man and maid."

Berry was a science teacher—hence the shark—and it's likely that her French teacher was Auguste Dantes Bellegarde, son of renowned Haitian diplomat, Dantes Bellegarde. Auguste and his wife, Oklahoma poet Ida Rowland, were both teaching at Langston where Josie was taking courses for her B.S. in Secondary Education. Poem republished, with *Southwester Anthology* credit, in *Ogden Standard Examiner*, Ogden, UT, 25 October 1942, p. 2. Berry was, at the time, living in Ogden, managing the Ogden Black USO. Berry worked in Junction City, Kansas, with their Black USO beginning 29 March 1943.

————. "An Ode to Washington." *The Black Dispatch*, May 13, 1921. Oklahoma Digital Newspaper Program. The Gateway to Oklahoma History, https://gateway.okhistory.org/.

Five Italian heroic quatrains. Author note: "Read at Recital of Portia Washington Pittman." Pittman was Booker T. Washington's daughter.

———. "And Death Went Down (To James Weldon Johnson)." In *Negro Voices: An Anthology of Contemporary Verse*, 13. New York: H. Harrison, 1938

Four Sicilian heroic quatrains. Header note to poem: "Mrs. Berry introduced James Weldon Johnson when he read two of his poems over and Oklahoma radio station during Poetry Week this year. It was shortly after that Mr. Johnson met his tragic death and Mrs. Berry dedicated her poem to him." Mr. Johnson spent two weeks in OKC (5-28 to 5-12-1938) during which time he gave the graduation speech for Douglass High School, met with the Scribblers writing group, and, as noted above, was featured on a WKY radio show with Berry introducing him. He died June 26, 1938.

———. "And Here's to You Governor Edwin P. Morrow." *The Black Dispatch*, February 21, 1920. Oklahoma Digital Newspaper Program. The Gateway to Oklahoma History, https://gateway.okhistory.org/.

Iambic pentameter. Structured as quatrain-triplet-quatrain; like a roundel but no refrain. Because the poem was squeezed into a short and narrow newspaper column, the lines and stanza breaks were determined by the rhyme and form. Kentucky governor Morrow "with a friendly legislature in 1920, [he] passed much of his agenda into law including an anti-lynching law and a reorganization of state government. He won national acclaim for preventing the lynching of a black prisoner in 1920. He was not hesitant to remove local officials who did not prevent or quell mob violence" (Morrow).

———. "Areopagitica." *The National Educational Outlook Among Negroes* 3, no. 3 Jan-Feb (February 1, 1940): 16

Four quatrains of unrhymed free verse. The poem follows the tradition of John Milton's pamphlet, *Areopagitica,* which was a defense of the right of freedom of speech and expression. The poem calls on Americans to speak out against lynching and racism. Berry names "the lilac-scented spinster of the ease," "the bigot in the black ecclesiastical robe," and "the narrow-minded drudge whose only spree / Rocks her in holy drunken ecstasy" among those who "do not wish to see / The sadists' funeral fire deep in the south."

———. "Awakening." *The Black Dispatch*, November 6, 1937, sec. Over My Shoulder. Center for Research Libraries, http://ddsnext.crl.edu/.

Unrhymed free verse. A poem about a young woman moving into adulthood. Its imagery and its concision, gives the poem a haiku-like aesthetic. last two lines: "Pear blossom and budding girl / twin mysteries.

———. "Ballad of Bill Malone." *The Black Dispatch*, August 12, 1939, sec. Over My Shoulder. The Oklahoma Historical Society Newspaper Archive.

Blues stanza (triplet), three beats to the line, rhymed AAA[Refrain]. The refrain consists of variations on "Before the war." Author note: "A ballad is usually a simple poem telling a tale of simple folk. It was one of the earliest forms of rhymed poetry. The modern ballad is a more elaborate poetic creation. In all forms of the ballad the trick of a repeated line or phrase comes from the old custom of singing ballads, hence, a refrain. 'The Ballad of Bill Malone' is our first effort at ballad-making, the last two stanzas being added twenty years after the original narrative." Berry reports that Kenneth Kaufman, in an article on ballads in his *Daily Oklahoman* literary column, states that "Stanley Vestal's 'Kit Carson's Last Ride' was 'the best modern Ballad in the English language'" ("Ballad"). Kaufman wrote, in the same column, that Oklahoma poet "Maurine Halliburton's ballad, 'After Supper' appeared in the SatEvePost July 1." The last two stanzas that she references in her author note are about WWII, with the final lines: That a scrap in Europe is a hell of a plan / To get DEMOCRACY for a colored man; But the lad will probably do all he can / In this next war." Used in the 14th stanza, term "Boche(s)" is "a contemptuous term used to refer to a German, especially a German soldier in World War I or II." Dictionary.com.

———. "Books." *The Black Dispatch*, November 16, 1933, 4. Center for Research Libraries, http://ddsnext.crl.edu/.

———. "Books." *The Black Dispatch*, October 29, 1937, sec. Over My Shoulder. Center for Research Libraries, http://ddsnext.crl.edu/.

The rhythm of this poem is complex, but scans as a variation on Anglo-Saxon prosody, with three stresses to each hemistich rather than four; the lines include strong caesuras. Rhyme is variable between stanzas but strict within: the first quatrain is AABB, the second ABAB, and the third, AABB. The final stanza is a triplet with attached couplet (ABBCC). "Books" is a song of praise for books and their ability to open minds. There are two very different versions of "Books" included in this text. The first (recovered in 2025) was published as a standalone work on 16 November 1933 in *The Black Dispatch,* p. 4. The second publication, 29 October 1937, p. 12, was a part of Berry's first Over My Shoulder (OMS) column.

———. "Death Towers." *Southwester* 1, no. Summer (July 1, 1937): 38

Blank verse. In her OMS column for January 15, 1938, Berry wrote: "We just missed greatness by a hair. At least two people have asked for an explanation of 'Death Towers,' which appeared on the literary page of *The Daily Oklahoman* December 5. If there had been a third we could not gave biased that we were writing stuff they could not understand. However, for fear our subtlety would never mystify three people simultaneously, we give this brief interpretation: Darkness was closing in, a storm was about to break, when out of the Northwest roared a plan headed for the landing field. It seemed that the plane was almost touching the housetops and I shuddered as I thought of the slender steel derricks between the pilot and safety. It seemed such a gallant thrilling race with Death. I could feel the pilot's tenseness as he was forced lower and lower keeping down under the ceiling of threatening clouds. The derricks did not stop the plane and I fancied reprisals in the lightning which has set more than one well afire. Later I wrote these lines . . ." (Berry quotes two stanzas of the poem). This poem won a prize from *Southwester*—reported in Kaufman's *Daily Oklahoman* column that featured the poem. Repub. in *Anthology of Poetry by Oklahoma Writers*, 1937, pg. 120.

———. "Dwindling Hopes." *Personal Notebook*, n.d., Circa 1968

Unrhymed, unmetered verse. In its expression of despair, the poem's tone resembles that of the Kennedy poems, so it was dated circa 1968.

———. "El Reno Evening." *The Black Dispatch*, July 23, 1938, sec. Over My Shoulder. Center for Research Libraries, http://ddsnext.crl.edu/.

Two combined long-measure (iambic pentameter) quatrains rhyming ABCB. A lovely imagistic portrait poem about sunset in El Reno, Oklahoma. El Reno is west of Oklahoma City, where Berry lived, and it is the portal to the Great Plains of western Oklahoma.

———. "Encroachment." *The Black Dispatch*, November 6, 1937, sec. Over My Shoulder. Center for Research Libraries, http://ddsnext.crl.edu/.

Scans as a Sapphic stanza, which is appropriate for the subject matter. A poem about the self-hatred of women who are mixed Black and white and their resultant hatred of Black people.

———. "Fall Housewife." *The Black Dispatch*, December 4, 1937, sec. Over My Shoulder. Center for Research Libraries, http://ddsnext.crl.edu/.

Two combined quatrains of long measure (iambic pentameter) rhyming ABCB. This poem is built on an extended metaphor of "Dame Winter" knitting an afghan of spring and summer to guard the earth from winter.

———. "Fire on the Mountain." *Personal Notebook*, n.d., Circa 1972

End rhymes in various stanza-positions: in 4 line stanzas #1 & #2, rhymes are lines 2 & 4. The third stanza, of five lines, rhymes lines 2 & 5. The final stanza of three lines concludes in an unmetered couplet. The poem's model line, closely adhered to, is two stresses per line. Perhaps written during the 1972 Riverside, CA fire. At the time, Berry was living there with one of her daughters.

———. "Frustration." *The Black Dispatch*, September 10, 1938, sec. Over My Shoulder. Center for Research Libraries, http://ddsnext.crl.edu/.

Four ABAB quatrains of 3 beat lines. Line four of each is an incremental frustrated-writer refrain built on "But, so far, I can't make the Post." One of four light verse poems published as a set. Author note: OMS presents some very light verse this week. We reserve the right to be the worst contributor of the column. However, there is on file some lighter verse that this, so if you see something of yours in print sometime, that you wonder why you write, don't blame OMS. The writing of parodies, limericks and other types of facetious verse and lines in the lighter vein is good practice for the student of poetry."

————. "Heritage." *The Black Dispatch*, November 13, 1937, sec. Over My Shoulder. Center for Research Libraries, http://ddsnext.crl.edu/.

 The poem's rhyme scheme suggests that it is built of three sestets in all in iambic pentameter. The first sestet is stanza 1; the second two are combined into stanza 2. A refrain, "Thank God I'm Black" is inserted at the beginning of stanza 1 and stanza 2; the refrain is also inserted after stanza 2. Sestets: The first is a heroic sestet rhyming ABBACC. The second sestet, rhyming AABCCD may be called a Dickinson sestet, since several of her poems display this rhyme scheme. The rhymes of the third sestet map to those in Yeats's "Wild Swans," except that the couplet is unrhymed.

————. "Home for Christmas." *The Black Dispatch*, December 25, 1937, sec. Over My Shoulder. Center for Research Libraries, http://ddsnext.crl.edu/.

 A single quatrain rhyming ABCB. Author note: "Thanks to Lloyd C. Douglas' book for title." Berry included a mini-review of Douglas's book in her column. Last line: "But what if there is no home?" A Great Depression comment hidden in a Christmas poem.

————. "I Am Not Done With Light." *Personal Notebook*, July 8, 1939

 Petrarchan sonnet. In an OMS column dated July 8, 1939, and in her notebook, Berry references "I Am Not done with Love" as one of a trilogy of sonnets. In her notebook list of contents, she enters the titles of the trilogy: "I Am Not Done With Love," "I Am Not Done With Light," and "I Am Not Done With Life." "I Am Not Done With Life" is hand-copied in her notebook. See bibliography entry for "I Am Not Done With Love." "I Am Not Done With Life" has not been recovered.

————. "I Am Not Done With Love." In *Eros: An Anthology of Modern Love Poems*, edited by Lucia Trent and Herbert Fouts, 160. New York: H. Harrison, 1939

 Undivided envelope sonnet ending in a couplet (ABBA CDDC EFEF GG). In an OMS column dated July 8, 1939, Berry calls this poem a sonnet trilogy; it is not published as a trilogy in the *Eros* anthology. She read the poem to faculty and fellow students while attending the OU Short Course in Professional Writing. Repub. in "Patterns in Poetry," a syndicated column by Sylvia Gardiner Lufburrow. (*The Central New Jersey Home News*, August 23, 1939).

————. "I Have No Tears To Shed." *Personal Notebook*, 1968

 "For Robert F. Kennedy." Unmetered verse with "ant end rhymes in each stanza (1 & 4, 1 & 3, 2 & 4). Stanzas are divided by two exclamatory lines, one after the first stanza, one after the second. In her notebook, Berry lists a "Kennedy Trilogy." The title of the third poem is "A Task Remains" for "E. K. '" Ethel Kennedy

————. "I Have Not Marched." *Personal Notebook*, n.d., Before 1968

"To Martin Luther King." A poem of "able feet: line 1, iambic pentameter; line 2, iambic heptameter. Stanzas two and four (lines 3-4 and 7-8), iambic hexameter; stanza three; iambic pentameter. In final couplet, the first line does not rhyme with any other end-word in the poem, but the second line rhymes with the previous couplet. This poem has been dated before 1968 for three reasons. First, the dedication line is "to" rather than "for" Second, the notebook's contents list includes a poem entitled "Who Leads the Throng Today" which is marked as an MLK poem. Finally, it does not read like an elegy which would have been the case after April 4, 1968.

————. "I Saw a Giant Fall." *Personal Notebook*, n.d., Circa 1970

Two quatrains of unmetered verse and an iambic tetrameter couplet. Last two lines of first stanza rhyme; second stanza is ABAB. The couplet is unrhymed. Likely written in the 1970s when Berry was living in Riverside, California with one of her daughters.

————. "In Memoriam." *The Black Dispatch*. May 2, 1919. Oklahoma Digital Newspaper Program. The Gateway to Oklahoma History, https://gateway.okhistory.org/.

Sicilian heroic sestet: iambic pentameter rhyming ABABAB. A memoriam poem for Berry's first child and only son, Henry Albert Berry, Jr. When he was eight years old (1918), he was "crossing the street late Friday evening just after supper when an automobile driven by a white man dashed into the child, crushing him to death under the wheels. He only lived a few minutes," *The Black Dispatch*, Friday, May 10, 1918.

————. "Is This Our World?" *The Black Dispatch*, December 18, 1937, sec. Over My Shoulder. Center for Research Libraries, http://ddsnext.crl.edu/.

Four octaves in syllabic verse lines alternating 8/4. Written in response to Paul B. Sears' environmental geology book entitled *This is Our World* which Berry reviews in her column. Last lines: "Man is a fool to think / He will endure, / He sits complacently, awhile / Sound and cocksure."

————. "June." *The Black Dispatch*, June 10, 1939, sec. Over My Shoulder. The Oklahoma Historical Society Newspaper Archive.

Seven line poem in two beat hemistiches rhymed ABABCDD. The final line is a full stich with four beats. If the last line were split like the others, the poem would be eight hemistiches. Berry followed the tradition of celebrating June as a month for marriage with this poem for lovers. "When fires spring up / in cheek and heart."

———. "Juneteenth." *The Black Dispatch*, June 18, 1938, sec. Over My Shoulder. Center for Research Libraries, http://ddsnext.crl.edu/.

Sonnet with Shakespearean rhyme scheme (ABAB CDCD EFEF GG but divided into octave and sestet, like a Petrarchan. According to the Encyclopedia of Oklahoma, Juneteenth celebrations were brought to Oklahoma as early as 1889 by Texas transplants. The novel manuscript that Oklahoman Ralph Ellison (a student of Berry's at OKC's Douglass High School) began in 1914 was called "Juneteenth." First two lines: "The sudden severing of enslaving chains / Made overtones to shouts of men made free."

———. "Lest You Forget!" *The Black Dispatch*, November 10, 1921. Oklahoma Digital Newspaper Program. The Gateway to Oklahoma History, https://gateway.okhistory.org/.

Long hymnal measure: three iambic tetrameter quatrains rhyming ABCB. Turning on a widely used WWI cultural phrase, this is a poem of mourning for Black soldiers killed in WWI. It asks that all Black Americans be treated equally. "Give their black babes a human's chance, / We ask again—Lest you Forget."

———. "Life in Oklahoma." *The Black Dispatch*, April 16, 1938, sec. Over My Shoulder. Center for Research Libraries, http://ddsnext.crl.edu/.

Sixteen lines composed in couplets. The standard line scans to cretic pentameter; amphibrach, dactyl, and anapest freely substituted. In her March 12, 1938 OMS, Berry writes, "I borrowed the beautiful rhythm of a Whitman title and sang our Southwest dust storms into a compact rhyme of sixteen lines." The Whitman title is likely "Out of the Cradle, Endlessly Rocking." See also note on "Out on the Prairie Wind, Easterly Blowing."

A dust bowl poem that reflects the tenacity of Oklahomans and their mode of speech. "This is home and we still like it, circumstances can't us lick;/ Gosh, an April snow is coming; grab that shovel, come on, quick!" Berry adds that the poem was a "Reprint from the *Times*, April 9, 1937." "The Times" likely refers to the Oklahoma City Times.

———. "Lilith-1937." *The Black Dispatch*, September 10, 1938, sec. Over My Shoulder. Center for Research Libraries, http://ddsnext.crl.edu/.

Three quatrains of three beats each; the first and third quatrains rhyme ABCB, the second, ABCC. One of four light verse poems published as a set. See note on "Frustration."

———. "Moderne." *The Black Dispatch*, September 10, 1938, sec. Over My Shoulder. Center for Research Libraries, http://ddsnext.crl.edu/.

Berry's unusual rhyme scheme in this poem (ABCCBADDA) maps perfectly to Robert Browning's "Natural Magic." Moreover, Berry's lines have the same number of beats (4/3) as Browning's. One of four light verse poems published as a set. See note on "Frustration."

————. "Nigger This, Nigger That." In *Self-Determination: The Salvation of the Race*, edited by J. H. A. Brazelton, 174–76. The Educator, 1918

The poem is written in perfect mockery of Kipling's "Tommy This and Tommy That: octaves of ballad meter, rhymed AABB in stanzas and AAAA in the refrains, It uses, for most of the poem, the same end-rhymes, sometimes substituting words that maintain the rhyme scheme rather than using Kipling's words. Berry's poem shifts in the penultimate octave. The first line of the octave is lifted directly from Kipling: "You talk o' better food for us, an' schools, an' fires, an' all." The concluding two lines of the octave refer to American wars. The final octave, a sestet with attached couplet, uses none of Kipling's end words.

The poem overtly states the attitude of many American Blacks of the period, that Black soldiers' sacrifices are a bargain with society, that, "If you'll only let us live in peace, we will show you how to die." Berry performed this poem in recital several times and *The Black Dispatch* reported it was well received. "Oklahoma City's brilliant Dramatic Artist and Author is now making a tour of the State in Recital. 'Nigger This, Nigger That,' one of Madam Berry's poems, is one of the most striking poems of the age. It vividly portrays the thralldom from which the Black man strives to rise and furnishes a splendid opportunity for her audience to see the careful, painstaking, sympathetic study that this Negro Woman has given to our social problems. Women's Clubs over the state and all church and fraternal organizations would do well to secure Madam Berry in recital" (*The Black Dispatch*, November 29, 1918).

————. "Nineteen Hundred Thirty Eight." *The Black Dispatch*, January 1, 1938, sec. Over My Shoulder. Center for Research Libraries, http://ddsnext.crl.edu/.

Structured as combined folk meter quatrains (podics 3/4/3/3). The title is a four-beat line as well. The first quatrain rhymes ABAB; the second is an envelope quatrain (CDDC). New Year's Day poem hoping for "the closing of a door / on past confusions."

————. "Oklahoma City." *The Black Dispatch*, April 22, 1939, sec. Over My Shoulder. The Oklahoma Historical Society Newspaper Archive.

Unrhymed trochaic tetrameter. Perhaps shows the influence of Longfellow's "The Song of Hiawatha," both in meter and in its song to a city "On a lake called Overholser." A poem of place, environment, culture, and history. Note in OMS indicates that the poem was first published in The Times, summer 1938. "The Times" likely refers to the Oklahoma City Times.

————. "Oklahombi." In *Anthology of Poetry by Oklahoma Writers*, 3:28. Oklahoma City, OK, 1937

Free verse. Author note: "Joseph Oklahombi, a Choctaw Indian, now living in Wright City, Okla., captured a nest of fifty (50) machine guns and trench mortars, single-handed, during the World War. He turned the guns on the enemy and held the position four (4) days under a heavy barrage. He took 171 prisoners. From *The Daily Oklahoman*, 1-17-37. Life has not been kind to Oklahombi" ("Oklahombi").

In October, 1937, the poem was featured in Elsie Parker's regionally-syndicated column, "The Poetry Corner" which was sponsored by the American Poetry Association (Wm. T. Hardy, Dallas). The association was chartered by the editors of Southwester. The syndicated poem was republished in the month of October in the following Oklahoma newspapers: *Adair County Democrat, Chickasha Star, Duncan Eagle, Haskell County Tribune, Sand Springs Leader,* and Stilwell's *Standard Sentinel.*

———. "Old Terra Firma." *Personal Notebook*, n.d., Circa 1974

Three stanzas rhymed ABAB. Although not in iambic meter, the poem approximates a folk ballad in form and in sound, when read aloud. A poem about air flight anxiety.

———. "One Royal Road." *The Black Dispatch*, September 10, 1938, sec. Over My Shoulder. Center for Research Libraries, http://ddsnext.crl.edu/.

This poem is a stave (drinking song). Three incremental couplet refrains, two ABAB quatrains. "Siwash" is a nickname for Knox College in Illinois. See also note on "Frustration."

———. "Out on the Prairie Wind, Easterly Blowing." In *Anthology of Poetry by Oklahoma Writers*, 4:26. Oklahoma City, OK: Mistletoe Press, 1938

There is no doubt that this is another poem influenced by Whitman, even more so than "Life in Oklahoma" (see entry). The rhythm of the title and its two repetitions sing the same song as "Out of the Cradle Endlessly Rocking." However, where Whitman's lines loosen into prosaics or hexameter, Berry's complex rhyme and meter continues throughout.

Poem composed four quatrains of three-stress tetrameter with patterned lines of iambic pentameter. ABCB. All B lines rhyme with B1 end rhyme, "there." Three-stress feet: dactylic, amphibrachic, anapestic. Repeated title lines (2) in dactylic tetrameter. Rhymes ABCB

In 1939, Berry's close friend, Louis L'Amour, published a poem entitled "Out of the Ocean Depths Soundlessly Moving" in his collection, *Smoke from this Altar*. Although he published regularly in small poetry magazines, this poem has not been documented as previously published in a journal. One wonders if Berry's poem and L'Amour's poem were written in a poetry challenge when they were both attending the 1938 OU Professional Writing Short Course.

Repub. in OMS, March 25, 1939, with this note: "This verse was written last year during the dust storms. It was published in the *Anthology of Oklahoma Writers* for 1938."

———. "Peace." *The Black Dispatch*, September 2, 1939, sec. Over My Shoulder. The Oklahoma Historical Society Newspaper Archive.

Four iambic pentameter heroic quatrains rhyming ABAB. The poem warns about the terrors of war and asserts that, "there will be peace / when men as brother's travel hand in hand." In OMS, the poem is associated with her (positive) review, of The Negro American Series of textbooks which was published in *The National Educational Outlook Among Negroes* in October, 1938

("Series"). She quotes from the book which encourages cooperation between blacks and whites in the US while acknowledging the place of blacks in the building of America. The Series was established and first written by Mrs. Emma E. Akin, "(white) supervisor of elementary grades in Drumright, Oklahoma," and was produced and printed by Harlow Publishing Corporation of Oklahoma City.

———. "Pray for Midnight." *Personal Notebook*, n.d., Circa 1968
    This unrhymed poem is divided into a six line first stanza and a five line second stanza. The model line's meter is three stresses. A prayer for the moral and spiritual awakening of a "brother different."

———. "Prayer for 1975." *Personal Notebook*, 1975
    Unrhymed unmetered verse. "A rendezvous with Death."

———. "River Home." *The Black Dispatch*, April 9, 1938, sec. Over My Shoulder. Center for Research Libraries, http://ddsnext.crl.edu/.
    Four quatrains in iambic octameter (like "The Raven") rhymed ABCB; seven eighth-foot amphimacer substitutions. Berry's note with this poem: "If the rhythm seems familiar, it's Poe. I do not mind borrowing it as he borrowed it from Mrs. Browning."

———. "Sanctuary." In *Anthology of Poetry by Oklahoma Writers*, 3:125, 1937
    Petrarchan sonnet; an Italian octave (ABBAABBA) and Sicilian quatrain (ABAB) ending with attached couplet. Uses, as an analogy for Black peoples' experiences, an extended metaphor of an eagle searching for a place to build a nest, but he can't find sanctuary. Berry states that this sonnet was not printed correctly in the *Anthology* and she included corrected version in OMS January 1, 1938. The corrected version is used for this project. Repub. in *The North America Book of Verse*, New York: H. Harrison, 1939, 265.

———. "Save." *The Black Dispatch*, March 7, 1920. Oklahoma Digital Newspaper Program. The Gateway to Oklahoma History, https://gateway.okhistory.org/.
    "A. Mitchell Palmer," (dedication line). Three combined quatrains of ballad measure (podics 4/3/4/3), rhyme ABAB. This poem is a critique of public exhortations to save money during the "Forgotten Depression" of 1920-21. Palmer is best known for overseeing the Palmer Raids during the Red Scare of 1919–20. However, in August 1919, President Wilson put him in charge of an anti-inflation campaign which the Lever Act, among other tactics, to put pressure on profiteers. He also organized a "housewives brigade" to report profiteers: "Palmer appealed to them to join his crusade 'to save America through an example of wise spending and frugal living'" ("Palmer"). Berry's poem points out that poor people—poor black people—don't have money to save and that Mitchell's campaign capitulated to business interests in 1920. The poem also

criticizes wealthy Blacks for not helping the Black community and those who make, sell, promote, and use skin whiteners.

———. "So Once Again, November." *The Black Dispatch*, November 26, 1938, sec. Over My Shoulder. Center for Research Libraries, http://ddsnext.crl.edu/.

A *Tempus Fugit* poem. Iambic pentameter. Two joined envelope quatrains rhyming ABBA.

———. "Song of Negro Club Women." *Half-Century Magazine* 7, no. 6 (December 1, 1919): 11

"Sung to the tune of 'America'" Official song of the Oklahoma Federation of Negro Women's Clubs. Repub. in *The Black Dispatch* as "Song of Oklahoma Club Women," 24 August 1922.

———. "Spring." *The Black Dispatch*, March 26, 1920. Oklahoma Digital Newspaper Program. The Gateway to Oklahoma History, https://gateway.okhistory.org/.

Four quatrains of long hymnal stanzas in iambic tetrameter rhyming ABAB. Spring as a symbol of resurrection.

———. "Spring Awakening." *The Black Dispatch*. March 18, 1939, sec. Over My Shoulder. The Oklahoma Historical Society Newspaper Archive.

Several different stanzas, lines, rhymes, and meters are merrily mixed in this humorous poem It uses parenthetical refrains in which the poet answers her previous stanza. However, even Berry's humorous poems carry cultural and political significance. In the last stanza of this poem, she references the Play Supreme (the Passion of Christ); it ends with this response, "(One Negro, Simon, got into one of these processions. You go home.)."

———. "Thanksgiving 1920." *The Black Dispatch*, November 26, 1920. Oklahoma Digital Newspaper Program. The Gateway to Oklahoma History, https://gateway.okhistory.org/.

Four quatrains of two couplets each (ABAB). All lines are fourteeners except the last lines of the first and last stanzas which are trochaic octameter and serve as a refrain. "We thank Thee, Lord that Black is Black and too that White is white; / We love our race integrity; preserve it by Thy might. / Yet there is neither Black nor White, Border, nor Breed, nor Birth, / When real men meet life face to face, tho they come from the end of the earth."

———. "Thanksgiving 1937." *The Black Dispatch*, November 27, 1937. Center for Research Libraries, http://ddsnext.crl.edu/.

Petrarchan sonnet; an Italian octave (ABBAABBA) and Sicilian quatrain (ABAB) ending with an attached couplet. Concluding couplet: "I'm thankful, Lord, the body, not the mind, / Was grounded by the fall of frail mankind." Repub. in *The North America Book of Verse,* New York: H. Harrison, 1939, 265.

———. "Thanksgiving 1970." *Personal Notebook*, 1970

    Dated November 15, 1970. Note indicates that this poem was published in the Press-Enterprise Parade. Another note reads, "Sent to L. Welk, in Escondido CA, June 26, 1976." This poem's model line is a two-stress cadence set in two four-line stanzas , perhaps mimicking the 2/4 time of the polka, Welk's signature form.

———. "The Children of the Sun." *The Black Dispatch*, March 14, 1920. Oklahoma Digital Newspaper Program. The Gateway to Oklahoma History, https://gateway.okhistory.org/.

    Four quatrains of three-beat lines rhyming ABCB. References Salem Tutt Whitney and J. Homer Tutt, "known collectively as the Tutt Brothers, were American vaudeville producers, writers, and performers of the late 19th and early 20th century. They were also known as Whitney & Tutt, Tutt & Whitney and the Whitney Brothers. They were prominent in black vaudeville and created over forty revues for black audiences" ("Tutt").

———. "The Dark Came Swiftly." *Personal Notebook*, 1963

    "For John Fitzgerald Kennedy." Unrhymed and unmetered elegy with one rhyming pair of lines: "grief" / "disbelief." In her notebook, Berry lists a "Kennedy Trilogy." See annotation for "I Have No Tears To Shed," the Robert F. Kennedy poem. The title of the third poem is listed in her notebook as "A Task Remains" for "E. K."—Ethel Kennedy. "A Task Remains" has not been recovered.

———. "The Devil Writes a Letter." *The Black Dispatch*, July 7, 1937. Center for Research Libraries, http://ddsnext.crl.edu/.

    Written in song measure (podics 4/3/4/3), rhyme ABAB. "To the Senate on the Anti-Lynching Bill" (dedication line). The devil speaks for the bill, in order to save the innocent and keep alive and working for him, the people who hate Blacks.

———. "The Female of the Species." *The Black Dispatch*, February 28, 1920. Oklahoma Digital Newspaper Program. The Gateway to Oklahoma History, https://gateway.okhistory.org/.

    "Apologies to Mr. Kipling" (dedication line). As with "Nigger This, Nigger That," this poem is modeled after Kipling's "The Female of the Species." However, Berry's poem is set in 4/2/4/2 beat lines instead of Kipling's 8/4/8/4 beat lines; the stanzas are likewise eight lines instead of Kipling's four. The lines were likely split to fit in to the narrow newspaper column. The poem topic is the old Irish tradition of women being allowed to ask men to marry them on Leap Year Day. Repub. in *The Black Dispatch*, 1924-02-07, page 8.

———. "The Mother Is a Friend Indeed." *The Black Dispatch*, May 7, 1938, sec. Over My Shoulder. Center for Research Libraries, http://ddsnext.crl.edu/.

    Two quatrains of ballad stanza. Josie's introduction of the poem from her *Black Dispatch* column, 7 May 1938: "Mother's Day always brings forth sweetness and sentiment. Fond recollections and a childhood smoother and tempered by my mother make me recall my first printed poem. It was titled THE MOTHER IS A FRIEND INDEED. It was a nine-days-wonder in the little Mississippi town when it appeared in the white paper and the nine-year-old (1897) author was asked to read it to an audience. I remember only two lines (sentences). The title was a refrain which bound together all the nice things a mother had done for her children. The mother who inspired the poem is still here." The remembered lines were published in OMS and are cited here.

———. "The Vicious Circle." *The Black Dispatch*, July 8, 1920. Oklahoma Digital Newspaper Program. The Gateway to Oklahoma History, https://gateway.okhistory.org/.

Three combined quatrains of ballad measure (podics 4/3/4/3), rhyme ABAB. The poem reveals the circle of blame that profiteers use to deny responsibility for high prices.

———. "The Winds of Chance." *Personal Notebook*, n.d., Circa 1975

This poem consists of two unmetered quatrains, an unmetered sestet, and a final, one-line plea. The first two stanzas have an interlocking rhyme scheme, while the sestet sets a new rhyme scheme, a single slant rhyme (like / live) in lines 3 & 6.

———. "This Thing Is Finished." *The Black Dispatch*, April 29, 1939, sec. Over My Shoulder. The Oklahoma Historical Society Newspaper Archive.

Unrhymed free verse. Incremental refrain of variations on "When we near the end of time." First two lines of second stanza: "these things go on until the end of time: / Antipathies of race and creed." This poem won second place in a national poetry contest sponsored by the 1940 American Negro Exhibition (Chicago). First place went to Melvin B. Tolson ("Negro Fair").

———. "To Robert Frost." *The Black Dispatch*, April 22, 1939, sec. Over My Shoulder. The Oklahoma Historical Society Newspaper Archive.

Unrhymed free verse. As reported in OMS, Robert Frost gave a reading in Edmond, OK on Saturday, April 22, 1939. Author Note: "When our poetry club was looking about for study material last year, Mrs. George R. Ragland suggested that we take up the work of some contemporary American poets. I was inspired to take Robert Frost for my individual study after hearing Mrs. Ragland read her favorite poem, 'Mending Wall.' I was intrigued by his poem 'The Sound of Trees' and attempted this answer."

———. "Toward Bethlehem." *The Black Dispatch*, December 24, 1938, sec. Over My Shoulder. Center for Research Libraries, http://ddsnext.crl.edu/.

Unrhymed free verse. When republished in 1942, "Toward Bethlehem" had been extensively revised from its 1938 text. The revised version will be used in this project because the poem's tightened lines and strengthened sonics result in a more polished poem. Moreover, it is the latest extant version of the piece. "The Star is there! / Oh earthborn, are you blinded?" Repub. in *The Ogden Standard-Examiner*, 23 December 1942, p. 2.

———. "Untitled." (*Twas only a face on a canvas). The Black Dispatch*. June 17, 1921, 5. Oklahoma Digital Newspaper Program. The Gateway to Oklahoma History, https://gateway.okhistory.org/.

Documenting the sources for Berry's untitled poem leads to a fascinting exploration longer than the poem itself. This untitled poem appears at the end of a review of two movies, *The Eyes of Youth* and *The Tiger's Coat*. *The Eyes of Youth* follows a young woman through visions of her future life as shown to her by a "Hindu's crystal." The young woman decides to choose love for her future rather than wealth or ambtion. *The Tiger's Coat* explores an interracial love affair. A white man, Alexander, and a young woman, Jean, who he thinks is related a Scottish friend of his, fall in love. Hyde, a man who is trying to ruin Alexander discovers that Jean is "low-born peon," a Mexican woman, then Alexander rejects her. Alexander later tries to approach her at an opera where she is performing but Jean rebuffs him. According to IMDB, the film "ranks as one of the more forward-thinking movies of 1920."

Berry combines elements of both films in her poem which also seems to refer to "The Face Upon the Barroom Floor," a song "first published in America in 1887" ("Barroom Floor"). The song has been performed through the years by well-known singers and otherwise referenced in pop culture: as a plotline Charlie Chaplin short film of the same title; Bob Hope related the entire poem in the film *Louisiana Purchase* (1941), and it is "indirectly referenced and/or alluded to multiple times in the 1996 novel *Infinite Jest* by David Foster Wallace" (Wikipedia). Berry was, yet again, ahead of her time, composing mixed-genre mash-ups in 1921.

———. "We're Here." *The Black Dispatch*. April 9, 1920. Oklahoma Digital Newspaper Program. The Gateway to Oklahoma History, https://gateway.okhistory.org/.

Three quatrains rhyming ABAB. Lines 1-3 anapestic / dactylic tetrameter. Line 4, iambic pentameter. Stanzas inferred by rhyme; when published it was squeezed into narrow and short column that made it look like prose. Critique of American companies hiring foreign workers at low wages then saying it's not fair when they can't find workers. Berry points out that here are many Black workers eager for a job but "their black skin shuts them in a doorless cage."

———. "What Do They Know?" *The Black Dispatch*, May 6, 1939, sec. Over My Shoulder. The Oklahoma Historical Society Newspaper Archive.

Author Note: "This is OMS's first short, short. Drop us a line if you like it." In July of 1938 and 1939, Berry attended the Short Course on Professional Writing (included fiction) at the University of Oklahoma.

———. "When Sunday Comes on Saturday." *The Black Dispatch*, June 4, 1920. Oklahoma Digital Newspaper Program. The Gateway to Oklahoma History, https://gateway.okhistory.org/.

Four quatrains of three-beat lines rhyming ABAB. Billy Sunday was famous pulpit evangelist who held tent revivals across America. He was an avowed Prohibitionist. Later in his career, with his wife as a partner, he built huge tabernacles in Detroit and New York City. He was a precursor to Jim and Tammy Faye Baker and Jerry Falwell, among others. Sunday and his wife are undoubtedly the inspiration for Upton Sinclair's novel, then movie, Elmer Gantry. In Berry's poem, Sunday is skewered for telling Black people that he'll evangelize them on Saturday because Sunday is reserved for white people ("Sunday").

———. "When We Greet the New Year." *Personal Notebook*, n.d., Circa 1970
A poem of three-stress lines rhyming ABCBA *Tempus Fugit* poem.

———. "Where Are the Children?" *Personal Notebook*, n.d., Circa 1975
Free verse. Although the lines of this poem vary from 9-12 syllables (with the exception of the fifth line), there's no identifiable meter or rhyme. It's likely the poem was written "by ear." This poem has been dated to 1975, because of its subject matter and also because the majority of poems in the notebook are dated to the 1970s. 1975 was the end of the Vietnam War and, although it's not mentioned explicitly—but the topic was on the minds of Americans.

———. "Where Are the Warring Brave?" *Southwester*. April 1, 1938
Spenserian sonnet. In her March 12, 1938 column, Berry says that she "spent a full half hour in determining the rhyme scheme of a Spenserian sonnet and writing one in which I changed only one word. I hope to get an award on it (from the Shakespeare Club) as it's much better than the verse that won last month which did not follow correctly the Spenserian form." Anti-war poem considering that soldiers' sacrifices were in vain. Last couplet: "They did not know—not one courageous heart— / We'd circle on the trail to near their start." Repub. in OMS, November 26, 1938. Repub. in *Sonnets* (anthology), Henry Harrison, 1939, page 52.

———. "Wind." In *Anthology of Poetry by Oklahoma Writers*, 3:103, 1937
Quatrain of iambic pentameter (ABAB) concluding with an unrhymed couplet. All Oklahoma poets have at least one wind poem; two by Berry have been identified. "The unleashed hounds of hell rush past the door" (2).

———. "Woe, Woe." *The Black Dispatch*, June 25, 1920, 4
Syllabic rispetto; two quatrains rhyming ABAB CCDD. Line varies between 10 and 12 syllables. "Rispetto" means "respect." Poem replying to a racial attack; the following is Berry's note: "At Wacross, Ga., a white Southerner passing thru the Jim Crow section of a train threw a lighted cigarette into the lap of a colored woman; when her husband spoke in protest, he was shot to death and left at a station. No attempt was made to arrest the white murderer."

Reference Bibliography

1880 United States Census. Rockhold, Whitley, Kentucky, digital image s.v. "J.S. Berry."

1900 United States Census. Clarksdale, Coahoma, Mississippi, digital image s.v. "Josie Berry."

1900 United States Census. Rockhold, Whitley, Kentucky, digital image s.v. "Henry Berry."

1910 United States Census. Oklahoma City, Oklahoma, Oklahoma, digital image s.v. "Henry Berry Jr."

Barr, Alwyn, and James M. Smallwood. "Juneteenth." In *The Encyclopedia of Oklahoma History and Culture.* Accessed January 20, 2022. https://www.okhistory.org/publications/enc/entry.php?entry=JU003.

Berry, Josie Craig. "Minutes of the Junction City, KS USO." U.S., Jewish Welfare Board, War Correspondence, 1917-1954, 1943. Ancestry.com. Document dates: 1943, March 29, April 5, April 12, April 18.

———. "Over My Shoulder." *The Black Dispatch*. November 20, 1937. Center for Research Libraries, http://ddsnext.crl.edu/.

———. "Over My Shoulder." *The Black Dispatch*. December 25, 1937. Center for Research Libraries, http://ddsnext.crl.edu/.

———. "Over My Shoulder." *The Black Dispatch*. January 15, 1938. Center for Research Libraries, http://ddsnext.crl.edu/.

———. "Over My Shoulder." *The Black Dispatch*. February 12, 1938. Center for Research Libraries, http://ddsnext.crl.edu/.

———. "Over My Shoulder." *The Black Dispatch*. April 2, 1938. Center for Research Libraries, http://ddsnext.crl.edu/.

———. "Over My Shoulder." *The Black Dispatch*. May 28, 1938. Center for Research Libraries, http://ddsnext.crl.edu/.

———. "Over My Shoulder." *The Black Dispatch*. June 11, 1938. Center for Research Libraries, http://ddsnext.crl.edu/.

———. "Over My Shoulder." *The Black Dispatch*. July 8, 1939. The Oklahoma Historical Society Newspaper Archive.

———. "Over My Shoulder." *The Black Dispatch*. July 29, 1939. The Oklahoma Historical Society Newspaper Archive.

———. "The Negro American Series." *The National Educational Outlook Among Negroes* 2, no. 2 (October 1938): 19–20.

Cooper, Brittney C. *Beyond Respectability: The Intellectual Thought of Race Women*. Champaign, Ill: University of Illinois Press, 2017.

Delashaw, Corie. "Oklahombi, Joseph." In *The Encyclopedia of Oklahoma History and Culture*. Accessed January 20, 2022. https://www.okhistory.org/publications/enc /entry.php?entry=OK091.

Fossedal, Gregory A. *Our Finest Hour: Will Clayton, the Marshall Plan, and the Triumph of Democracy*. Stanford, CA: Hoover Institution Press, 2013.

"Freddye Harper Williams." In *Who Is Who in the 42nd Oklahoma Legislature*, 48. Oklahoma City, OK, 1989. Archives.OK.Gov. Oklahoma Digital Prairie.

Hanrahan, John. "Decline of a Presidency: Woodrow Wilson and the Inflation Issue, 1919-1920." Faculty Research at Morehead State University, January 1, 1982, 13. https:// scholarworks.moreheadstate.edu/msu_faculty_research/62.

Hart, Henry. *The Writer in a Changing World*. London, 1937.

IMDB Contributors. *The Tiger's Coat*. In *Internet Movie Database* (IMDB). Accessed August 3, 2025, https://www.imdb.com/title/tt0188237/.

Kaufman, Kenneth C. "Maurine Halliburton Lifts An Oklahoma Ballad to the Peak of Literary Excellence." *The Daily Oklahoman*. July 30, 1939, Sunday edition, sec. An Oklahoma Angle on Important Things Literary. Newspapers.com.

———. "Poetry." *The Daily Oklahoman*. December 5, 1937, Sunday edition, sec. An Oklahoma Angle on Things Literary. Newspapers.com.

Knoxville College. "Knoxville College Bulletin." Knoxville, TN, June 1906. HathiTrust. https://catalog.hathitrust.org/Record/100679386.

———. "Knoxville College Bulletin." Knoxville, TN, March 1907. HathiTrust. https://catalog.hathitrust.org/Record/100679386.

———. "Knoxville College Bulletin." Knoxville, TN, March 1908. HathiTrust. https://catalog.hathitrust.org/Record/100679386.

Oklahoma County Marriage Records, 1889-1951. Oklahoma City, OK: 06-01-1909, digital image s.v. "Josie B. Craig."

Oklahoma City Times. "One-Day College Head Found but Won't Talk." October 13, 1939. Oklahoma Digital Newspaper Program. The Gateway to Oklahoma History, https://gateway.okhistory.org/.

Oklahoma City Times. "Poet to Speak." April 20, 1939. Oklahoma Digital Newspaper Program. The Gateway to Oklahoma History, https://gateway.okhistory.org/.

The New York Age. "Poetry Contest for American Negro Fair Won By Wiley Prof." June 6, 1940. Newspapers.com.

Smith, Beverly. "King Cotton." *The American Magazine,* April 1938.

Sooner State Press. "316 Persons Come to Writers' Course." July 16, 1938. Oklahoma Digital Newspaper Program. The Gateway to Oklahoma History, https://gateway.okhistory .org.

St. Louis Birth Registers, 1888-1889. St. Louis, MO: 11-17-1888, digital image s.v. "Female Craig." Ancestry.com.

Strong, Willa Allegra. "The Origin, Development, and Current Status of the Oklahoma Federation of Colored Women's Clubs." Dissertation, University of Oklahoma, 1957. ShareOK. https://shareok.org/handle/11244/249.

Terrell, Mary Church. 1898. "The Progress of Colored Women." Digital facsimile. Library of Congress. https://www.loc.gov/item/90898298/.

The Black Dispatch. "Douglass News." May 21, 1938. The Oklahoma Historical Society Newspaper Archive.

———. "National Poetry Week." May 28, 1938. Center for Research Libraries, http://ddsnext.crl.edu/.

———. "Writers Congress in Session at YWCA." May 27, 1937. Center for Research Libraries, http://ddsnext.crl.edu/.

Metropolitan (Oklahoma City) Library System. "Douglass High School—Leading Educational Institution." Archives Essay. Accessed June 12, 2025. www.metrolibrary.org/archives/essay/2019/07/douglass-high-school-leading-educational-institution

"The Official Register of Harvard University." Summer School of Arts and Sciences. Cambridge, MA: Harvard University, May 2, 1910. Google Books. https://www .google.com/books/edition/Official_Register/HIY4AAAAMAA.

The Ogden Standard-Examiner. "Negro USO Ends Holliday Season." January 3, 1943. Newspapers.com.

———. "Social Worker Voices Praise." October 18, 1942. Newspapers.com.

Thomson, John H. L. "Dunjee, Roscoe (1883-1965)." In *The Encyclopedia of Oklahoma History and Culture*. Accessed January 21, 2022. https://www.okhistory.org/publications/enc /entry.php?entry=DU007.

The White House. "Warren G. Harding." In Wikipedia, August 15, 2023. https://www .whitehouse.gov/about-the-white-house/presidents/warren-g-harding/.

Wikipedia contributors. "Billy Sunday." In Wikipedia. Accessed January 21, 2022. https://en .wikipedia.org/wiki/Billy_Sunday.

———. "Boche." (List of terms used for Germans.) In Wikipedia."https://en.wikipedia.org/wiki/List_of_terms_used_for_Germans#Boche

———. "Coleman Livingston Blease." In Wikipedia, January 9, 2022. https://en .wikipedia.org/wiki/Coleman_Livingston_Blease.

———. "Edwin P. Morrow." In Wikipedia. Accessed January 20, 2022. https://en.wikipedia.org/wiki/Edwin_P._Morrow.

———. "Jackson Barnett." In Wikipedia. Accessed October 25, 2021. https://en.wikipedia .org/wiki/Jackson_Barnett.

———. "James K. Vardaman." In Wikipedia. Accessed January 27, 2022. https://en .wikipedia.org/wiki/ James_K._Vardaman.

———. "List of Terms Used for Germans." In Wikipedia. Accessed February 9, 2022. https:// en.wikipedia.org/wiki/List_of_terms_used_for_Germans.

———. "Lynching of John Carter." In Wikipedia. Accessed February 12, 2022. https:// en .wikipedia.org/wiki/Lynching_of_John_Carter.

———."The Face Upon the Barroom Floor." Accessed August 15, 2023. https://en.wikipedia.org/wiki/ The_Face_upon_the_Barroom_Floor.

———. "Tutt Brothers." In Wikipedia. Accessed January 21, 2022. https://en.wikipedia.org /wiki/ Tutt_Brothers.